UNCOMMON

INSIDE MY COACHING CAREER AT
SACRAMENTO WALDORF

DEAN STARK

UNCOMMON

INSIDE MY COACHING CAREER AT SACRAMENTO WALDORF

print ISBN: 978-1-09835-480-0

CONTENTS

ACKNOWLEDGEMENTS

First I want to thank the original Stark family:

Dad — You passed away when I was 9, but my life has been fueled to make you proud. I hope I have.

Mom — Your unconditional love and support for all of your sons is abundantly evident. We are all blessed to have you guide our family.

Brothers — Randy, Terry, Cris:

Randy — All us brothers have felt your leadership over the years. You've played a big part in keeping us connected. Thank you.

Terry — You're the best coach I know. Thank you for setting an extraordinarily high bar to chase after as an athlete and a coach.

Cris—- Closest in age to me meant we fought a lot, but it also meant we did the most together. I miss those days.

My new Stark family:

Aimee — Being married to you has been the greatest gift of my life. Thank you for these past five years. You mean the world to me.

Famy — I spent most of my adult life wondering what it would be like to have a son or daughter. You entered my world and my dream came true. I love you.

My Waves family — All of you who I've coached. 34 basketball teams, 16 baseball teams, and even four volleyball teams. I can't thank you enough for your commitment, effort, respect and friendship. You have impacted my life deeply.

Students I've sponsored — Classes of '96, '98, '00, '04, '08, '12, '16, and '20. To have the opportunity to share your high school experience is something I only could have done at a Waldorf school. It's all been one of the greatest gifts of my life.

The Waldorf community at large — Supporting me and cheering on my teams has meant a lot. You've embraced our program and helped make it a shining part of our school. Thank you.

Assistant coaches — There are too many to mention by name, but thank you for your commitments to me and the program. None of this is possible without all of your efforts.

DEDICATION

This book is dedicated to all of my players, past and present. You have given me far more than I can ever hope to repay. You've been my teacher and my inspiration. The memories we've shared have filled my heart for a lifetime.

FOREWORD

I recall being down big early in the fourth quarter. It was embarrassing and disheartening and there was no comfort in the fact we were playing a large public high school. Returning to the bench dejected because their second string was being put in, one of my teammates found a way to lighten the mood, "Maybe they have hops, but can they knit?"

The image of Waldorf brings up many things for many people, but basketball powerhouse is not usually among the first connotations. For those tied to the Sacramento-area sports scene, however, Dean Stark is a highly-respected coach intimately connected to basketball. He has coached at Sacramento Waldorf for over three decades, notched over 600 wins, and influenced countless numbers of students both on and off the court.

During the four years from 2009 to 2012 that I played for Dean, we garnered a lot of attention as a very small private school that achieved remarkable success. We won a total of 88 games with 27 losses and had an overall league record of 39-9. In our final season together we won the league championship with an undefeated record. Our team was not the first to accomplish this feat under Dean's direction, nor the second or the third, but the sixth.

Possibly even more incredible than these statistics is that Dean is able to put up these numbers given the fact that in any given season the guys on the floor may include players new to the game. When other coaches are holding tryouts, Dean is convincing people they would enjoy the sport if they gave it a try. This reveals Dean's true talent: He takes the group he is given and weaves together a cohesive whole.

The relationship between a player and coach is a very complex one, as each individual has a very different perspective on the game. Most players have reasons why a mistake happens. Playing basketball means processing a hundred things at any given time. But the coach has the singular job of making sure mistakes don't happen again. So when a player feels they have a legitimate reason for why something occurred, and the coach doesn't want to hear it — "no excuses, no explanations"— there is an obvious potential for conflict. It would be easy for players to harbor resentment and lose trust with the coach. After all, a player can be right — there are often legitimate reasons for the breakdown.

When the relationship is built on trust, however, the player understands where the coach is coming from. The player does not receive criticism and silently stew, there is an understanding and a motivation to adapt and problem solve in order to mitigate future mistakes.

This trust Dean creates, coupled with his emotional intelligence, helps him strike an amazing balance between disciplinarian and friend. He knows exactly how hard he can push certain players — he knows who needs a bit more encouragement, who he can tease, and when he needs to do it. He understands that sometimes silence can be louder than yelling and that a joke can be more effective than a critique. Off the court, it did not matter if we won the night before or suffered a horrible loss: Dean was there to support us.

Another trait that stands out to me is the passion Dean brings to his team. I have never seen another coach run up and down the sidelines to follow the play or jump up in the air as the ball came off the rim as if to grab the rebound himself. It is inspiring knowing your coach is as invested in the game as you are. He is present in every moment, battling right alongside you.

What I respect most about this part of Dean is the authenticity of his passion. It is easy to bring that energy in your first couple years of coaching, but it is damn near impossible after 30-plus years. But he still brings the same intensity on day 10,095 as he did on day one, because it is the same fire that drives him: his thirst to win. Dean is the ultimate competitor, but that alone does not make a coach great. It is his incredible ability to unlock this competitive desire in his players — regardless of their talent, experience, or previous level of interest in athletics — that makes him special. Soon, even those new to the game want to be the first to dive on the floor for loose balls and take charges in the pursuit of victory.

It is not just Dean's passion that inspires players, but the lessons he imparts to his teams. Every year Dean brought a theme that would be the foundation that we built our seasons on, a mantra we could unite over and fall back on when things got difficult.

My freshmen year the theme was "Toughness Tuesday." Every Tuesday when we walked in the gym we knew it was going to be hell. It was two hours of conditioning and defensive shell drills that had to be executed perfectly or we would have to run — continuing that cycle until we got it right. Personally, I dreaded Tuesdays, but as a young freshman I always felt prepared for games because nothing we faced would be as difficult as those practices.

Sophomore year was "Wolf Pack." Like a wolf pack, we had seven guys on the team and our goal was to hunt together day in and day out. We were seven individuals that came together to work as a single unit. We were the aggressors, attacking our prey when we sensed they were weak. With this mentality we vastly overachieved and, despite not winning the league championship, it is the season I look back on with the fondest memories because of how close we were as a group.

Junior year "Kaizen" — Japanese for "continuous improvement" — was our theme. Dean has since confided in me that he had very low expectations for our team going into that season. Having graduated three key starters from the year before, we were a ragtag group — our starting center was playing basketball for the first time ever. Day in and day out we worked — not with the goal of perfection, but with the goal of being better than we were the day before. By the end of the season, we were playing our best basketball, narrowly missing a league title and finishing second overall in the standings.

My senior year our motto was "Sacrifice for the Unknown." At the start of the season, Dean posed a scenario for us: Would it be easy to work as hard as you can, every single day for six months if at the end of that time you were guaranteed a reward for your efforts? But would you still do it if the outcome was not guaranteed? We committed even though our results were not assured. We gave everything we had that season in both practice and games and achieved tremendous success, winning the league title undefeated.

It would be easy to say that Dean is a remarkable coach — the best I have ever played for — because of the memories he helped create. That, however, would only be half the truth. Dean was the best coach I ever played for because he imparted wisdom beyond the sport. I became a better basketball player under Dean's tutelage, but more importantly, a better person.

—Chris Schwartz-Edmisten, Class of 2012

LAST TWENTY YEARS

After climbing a great hill, one only finds that there are many more hills to climb.

—Nelson Mandela

Right around the year 2000, I wrote a book titled *A Waldorf Approach To Coaching Team Sports*. I'm proud to say that it was very well received. I heard from people all over the world who shared with me how it had inspired and impacted their lives and coaching philosophies. Fast forwarding to 2020, it's amazing to think that 20 years has gone by since the publication of that first book. So much has happened in the interim. I'm now in my 36th year at Sacramento Waldorf and recently completed my 34th season as the boys varsity basketball coach. Whew!

In 2000, I never would have dreamed that I wasn't even half way into my coaching career. I never thought about it at length, but at that time I didn't see myself coaching into my 50's. I did, however, always believe and state that passion had to live first and foremost in what one was doing. I knew that if I felt my fire and enthusiasm waver at all, it would be time to step away. I believe one owes it to his or her players to give everything he or she has everyday. Well, I'm still here and still searching and developing ways to maintain that fire, passion and enthusiasm.

In recent months, I started to contemplate writing a follow up to my original book. I would jot down topics just in case I decided to share my thoughts again. Finding time for a project like this, however, is always a hugely daunting task. There never seems to be the perfect moment to sit down and just begin. But that has changed.

Coronavirus...Covid-19. The pandemic has disrupted our normal routines and left gaping holes in many of our typically jam-packed schedules.

In Fair Oaks, California — like everywhere else in the world — we are learning new terms like social distancing, self-isolation, self-quarantine, and shelter-at-home. People are being asked to hunker down. While the virus' impact has created much hardship, it has actually been a great opportunity to take advantage of a very scary time in the world and focus on something positive. If I can't find time to write now, then when?

So that is what I am doing.

In this book, I will be sharing my coaching career with you from 2000 to the present, giving the reader an up close view of how things have changed, and the steps I've taken to continually strive to be the best that I can be.

First, though, a recap. In 2000, truth be told, Sac Waldorf was in the midst of a talent shortage. I honestly didn't know if we would ever be champions again. We were coming off a subpar '99 season, and looking into the immediate future didn't give me much hope either. We had won five league titles in the 90's, but that looked like a distant memory heading into the new millenium.

The first couple years of the decade were lean. In 2002 I only had six players on our varsity team. This group battled admirably, though, and we finished tied for second in league, and advanced to the playoffs. We went into the postseason as the No. 15 seed and had to travel to Turlock to face the No. 2 seed, Turlock Christian. Somehow, we put together our greatest performance of the year and came away with a huge upset win. It kept alive a string of winning at least a first round playoff game every year since 1994. That streak would ultimately extend all the way to 2015.

Entering into the 2003 season, I knew things were changing talent-wise and slowly I could feel the pressure of expectations growing inside me. Everyone thinks there's more stress when you are coaching a team that doesn't win much, but honestly — at least for me — the teams that have lower expectations are far less stressful to coach.

After the first few weeks of practice, it was evident that this was going to be the best team I had since the early 90's. We had a chance to be champions. It had been four years since we had won a league title and I felt like if I was ever going to get another one, it was with this group.

Well, we won that title with an undefeated league championship. We followed it up with a championship in 2004 as well. The pressure I put on myself to produce was real, though. After the 2004 campaign, I was burnt out and needed a break. I had coached 19 consecutive seasons and I truly thought I might be done. I was extremely satisfied that I got my team back to the top and I felt like it was a perfect time to step away. It was time to see if my coaching career was complete.

2005, however, was brutal. As athletic director, I had to be at all of our home games. Watching my guys on the floor and not being on the sidelines with them was very hard. We had a talented team and it was impossible for me to not think of what I could do with that group. This experience, however, was very valuable for me: it proved that I missed coaching deeply and had a lot more to give. It also gave me more time to contemplate how I could improve as a coach, and how I could make it a healthier experience for me and my players.

I attacked 2006 with tremendous preparation and enthusiasm. It also didn't hurt that I had a very talented team. We raced through the season undefeated in league play and finished with a 25-2 record. To this day it's still my best win/loss percentage for any season. Our only two setbacks were to much bigger schools.

2007 was fairly similar. Another league championship and postseason success, but the year was marred by an unbelievably tragic loss of life of one of my players, Jarrad Cole. This incredibly sad event jolted our community — and yet it brought us even closer together, uniting us as one in an effort to help support his family in grieving for a very special young man. I will share more thoughts on Jarrad in a later chapter.

As in 2000, when 2008 approached I could see that our talent had dipped. We lost seven or eight very good players over the past couple of seasons. I was on a personal four year championship run, though, and thought anything was possible.

Over the next four years, we would compete hard but never could quite get to the championship level. We still made the playoffs each season, and won at least one playoff game every year, but the ultimate prize always eluded us.

As 2012 approached, I knew we would be formidable because I had a veteran team with battle-tested seniors. I also knew that I had a young man who was special. Chris Schwartz-Edmisten was a four-year starter for me and had averaged 30 points a game as a junior. In my 34 years coaching basketball, Chris stands alone as the best I ever coached. Chris put the team on his back that season and carried us to an undefeated league championship — 27 wins, and a final four appearance in the CIF Section and the NorCal playoffs. He finished the season averaging 34 points a game (4th best in the country) and ended his high school career scoring over 2,400 points — putting him 7th all time in the history of the CIF. He was truly a once in a generation player.

After Chris graduated, the void he left was gigantic. He did almost everything for our team and there really wasn't anyone to fill the void he left. The next two years were a huge struggle. We finished 26-26 over those two seasons and missed the playoffs each time. The only other year we hadn't made the postseason since the mid-80's was 1999.

However, things felt differently then they did in 2000. I could look into the future and see real potential. The 9th and 10th graders in 2013 and 2014 had that look. After a couple of injury setbacks that stalled our 2015 season, I entered 2016 confident that we were ready to challenge again for the title. My vision proved accurate as we were champions in 2016.

2017, '18 and '19 followed the same script. It was the third time in our school's history that we had won at least four consecutive league titles — all in different decades. In our league's history, no other school has won more than two titles in a row. We also had back-to-back undefeated league seasons in 2017 and '18. No other school has ever done that either — except for us in '91 and '92.

2017 was also a year of unbelievably humbling recognition. I was the recipient of the CIF Sectional and State Model Coach Awards for Basketball. These honors go to the coach who best demonstrated and taught the six core ethical values: trustworthiness, respect, responsibility, fairness, caring, and good citizenship (the "Six Pillars of Character").

I also received the National Federation of State High School Associations (NFHS) California — State Boys Basketball Coach of the Year. To me, this was recognition for having a great team.

I finished my 34th season this past February, and in that span the Sacramento Waldorf Waves have won 16 league titles. It's been a truly amazing run. The school closest to us by this measure has six.

This summary just gets you up to date on the success of our program the past three-plus decades. Yes, we have won a lot, but what I really want to focus on is the how and the why.

Former player Tyson Duncan's wardrobe

The Sac Waldorf Way

When I'm asked how my Sacramento Waldorf team is successful year after year with such a small pool of athletes to draw from, I say it's our approach to sports. We have high expectations. We hold players accountable. We have a philosophy of sport — the why, the how. We show them what playing on a team can ultimately mean.

Instead of dedicating one's life to sport, I want my players to dedicate their sport to life.

In this era of ultra-competitive youth sports, it's difficult to find a balance between win-at-all-costs and playing for enjoyment. Is the goal to teach children to just endure competition? Is it to prepare them for a competitive work world? Maybe, but competition, fostered properly, can also be a wonderful developmental aid. It can help foment a passion for an activity, and better prepare students to work well with others.

Competitive sports should invigorate and inspire, not create anxiety and stress. Drawing from Waldorf philosophy and personal experience, I strive to highlight the benefits of being part of a team and enjoying a sport for the beauty of playing it.

There are a couple of other hurdles that every program needs to address when it comes to building a successful team — playing time and cuts. The tryout and cut or no-cut policy is certainly a hot topic in youth sports. Being cut from a team can emotionally scar a kid. But getting cut can also motivate someone to great heights. While a no-cut policy doesn't give one the sense of earning anything, it affords anyone the opportunity to participate.

I see both sides. As a small school, we don't have tryouts for our team. Every student is welcome. I have seen kids that never would have had an opportunity to play at a bigger school get a chance, excel, and even make it at the college level. It's rare, but it happens. At another school, these same kids would have gotten cut in 9th grade and never would have set foot on the court again. That's the beauty of our approach.

Even though we don't have tryouts, we do have our own way to make sure athletes earn their roster spot. My basketball players all must run a mile, a two mile, and a quarter-mile under a specified time. It's challenging but doable. In 15 years of setting this bar, every kid has qualified. Sometimes it takes multiple efforts to achieve the desired time, but persistence pays off. I've witnessed the sense of accomplishment and camaraderie when teammates cheer on one of their own. Student athletes who don't think they can do it still press forward because of the unwavering support of their brothers and sisters.

These types of benchmarks truly help build a sense of family. They also develop a feeling of "I earned this," and that's a piece that can be missing when everyone can just freely join in.

Another important issue is playing time. In our community, we have a group that believes everyone should get to play regardless of skill level. We also have a faction that thinks the best players should play, period. Again, I see both sides. Playing everyone can foster enthusiasm *and* resentment.

Should a player get equal or similar playing time even though they aren't nearly as committed or talented? Should a player not get time on the court or field even though they have a phenomenal work ethic and attitude?

My philosophy — at the varsity level — is that no one is guaranteed playing time. Showing up to practice every day on time, hustling, and maintaining a positive attitude only gives a player the opportunity to play. Skill on the court does matter.

Meeting with parents before the season — and meeting individually with each player to define his or her role with the team — goes a long way toward alleviating potential friction.

There can be many ways to weigh the success of a program: winning, losing, level of participation, and enthusiasm, to name a few. I believe we have a strong program because everyone gets the opportunity to play, our players genuinely care, and our coaches help make the experience special.

Navigating playing time, cuts, commitment, effort, and enthusiasm are many of the elements that build a school's foundational philosophy. And if balancing these elements is the bar by which one determines a school's successes, then I'd say we're hitting home runs.

COMPETITION— WHAT'S CHANGED?

The ultimate victory in competition is derived from the inner satisfaction of knowing that you have done your best and that you have given the most out of what you had to give.

—Howard Cosell

Eventually you learn that the competition is against the little voice inside you that wants to quit.

—George Sheehan

In my first book, *A Waldorf Approach To Coaching Team Sports*, I spoke about competition in a Waldorf School environment and age appropriateness. The success of the Waves' teams I coached in the 90's garnered attention in the Waldorf community at large and when I would talk to teachers and coaches at other schools there were invariably questions about the program. From my first book:

> Wherever and whenever I visited a Waldorf school, people there knew of our basketball team, and in my conversations with these people, two recurring topics kept popping up: first, "how did you do it and how can we do it," and second, "how does one deal with the dreaded "C" word — competition — which we don't want encouraged here?"

Twenty years later, I still field calls from all over the world about how to start a program. Continuing these conversations has been one of the biggest gifts in writing the first book. And, based on the continued dialogue, it seems there's less concern about competition, which isn't brought up nearly as much as it once was. In Waldorf circles, organized sports seem to be far more accepted nowadays.

That doesn't mean that there isn't some hand-wringing with regard to competition, and the concerns from 20 years ago are still valid today. In *A Waldorf Approach To Coaching Team Sports* I looked to Rudolf Kischnick, who was one of the first to apply Waldorf education founder Rudolf Steiner's pedagogical lessons to physical education. He wrote in his book *Games, Gymnastics, Sports in Child Development* that:

> The standard for achievement is the effort. If the pupil does not need to make an effort, he is not conscious of the fact that he has achieved something. In order to let him develop these capacities, a certain opposition should be put in his way. Exactly in the time between the ninth and eleventh school years the growing human being likes to come to terms with the problems of opposition. For if one does not offer him the opportunity for this now, he will later become undisciplined, when it is important for him to conquer inner oppositions. Also within oneself one has to overcome many obstacles, before one reaches one's value, and not for nothing does destiny give one the opportunity to do, outwardly, during youth, what later has to bring into practice inwardly.

A perfect example of this effort that Kischnick talks about is the conditioning I put my players through. Instead of just receiving their jersey because there are no cuts, my guys have to run a quarter mile, and a one and two miler under a certain time to earn playing time in a game.

Trust me, my players are fully conscious that they have achieved something special when they qualify for all three runs. There is definitely a sense of pride in earning their spot on the team.

As I said in my previous book:

Brought in the right way, competition can accomplish this. It helps create an avenue for students to be truly passionate about something in their lives. Competition doesn't have to be about winning. I virtually never talk to my players about winning. I always stress playing to their best ability and giving everything that they are capable of. If they do these and practice correctly, winning will take care of itself.

Visiting Age Appropriateness

In 2000, the National Youth Sports Coaches reported that nearly 20 million children play a team sport before high school. Of that number, 75 percent who start at age six or seven will quit before they are 15.

Twenty years later the numbers are still similar. Although the total number of children playing a team sport has skyrocketed to 45 million, the percentage that will quit by 15 is right around 80 percent. Very little change. Why is this trend still steady two decades down the road?

Turning to Kischnick again, he says it is vital to develop a healthy relationships with physical activity in a way that shapes both the body and mind:

There are worlds of difference that lie between the single years of life… In the second seven year period of the child, he starts off with beauty and harmony. The responsibility of the teacher or coach for the young people in his care, when keeping this perspective in mind, is obviously very great. He needs to teach in a way that brings reverence to the child's virtues. All physical education has to be at the same time moral education. If one allows children to play sports while moral forces do not carry the movement, one surrenders them to the forces of the earth.

The body hardens, the heart wastes away and the spirit dries up.

In taking in Kischnick's words, one can see the importance coaches play in bringing competition to children in a healthy way. If they are pushed to win at all costs or just drilled repetitively to improve fundamentals, most kids will ultimately end up as a part of that burn out statistic.

At Sacramento Waldorf, we have evolved a bit in the past twenty years. In 2000, we allowed organized participation starting in the 7th grade. Now, our 6th graders get to play as well. It's been a huge success, so much so that there has been a little push to lower it down even into the 5th grade as well. It is already happening at a couple of nearby Waldorf schools, but so far we have resisted.

I understand the temptation. Many families all around us have their children in organized sports, some much younger than 11, and many fifth graders here are already chomping at the bit to play. I still see both sides.

I do believe one can have a healthy and safe experience participating in organized sports at an early age, but I also believe there is a risk in your child encountering an activity that is not taught in a way that brings reverence to your child's virtues as well.

I also can't say that every coach I've hired at Waldorf has been the ideal role model for fostering moral education. There are no guarantees.

I can tell you that our participation numbers in our middle school are through the roof. We had 80 percent of our 6th through 8th grade students play at least one sport. At the high school level in 2019, our numbers were right at 70 percent.

Allowing our 6th graders to compete doesn't seem to have hurt our high school participation thus far, and it has surely boosted the enthusiasm of our 12-year olds. All in all, my advice is to hire the best coaches possible, pay them an appropriate stipend, give them clear guidelines and expectations, and encourage them to immerse themselves into the Waldorf pedagogy and community.

Great Coaches Make a Great Difference

But what about competition, period? What is our stance today as a nation? As controversial as it has been at Waldorf schools, I would say it has been comparable around the world as well. There certainly has been a push in recent years to downplay competition. There are youth leagues popping up all over that don't keep score, and where everyone gets a participation trophy or medal.

That, in itself, has spawned huge arguments about how this mindset is serving our youth. Again, I see both sides. I do have concerns about the "everyone gets a trophy" mentality. What are we encouraging? Potentially, it could lead to less effort, less commitment, less caring, and even less enjoyment.

On the flip side, winning at all costs isn't the answer either. The "winning isn't everything, it's the only thing" mantra could be similarly damaging. This is where the artistry of coaching is so important.

Coaches, I believe, need to preach certain ideals: striving to win, giving it your best, and sacrificing in order to achieve success. These principles should be emphasized over the "everyone gets a medal" or the "win or else" mindsets.

If a coach can instill these traits into the players of today, they will help to ensure life-long lessons that their players can take with them as they enter adulthood and the workplace. I know my former players have commented often about the lessons they learned on the court and how that impacted and shaped their personal and professional lives.

LIVING YOUR PHILOSOPHY

You cannot build a dream on a foundation of sand. To weather the test of storms, it must be cemented in the heart with uncompromising conviction.

—T.F. Hodge

In *A Waldorf Approach To Coaching Team Sports* I spoke about my coaching philosophy throughout the book. Whether I was talking about motivating players, striving to win, or how to schedule a practice, I shared my beliefs and what worked well for me.

At that time, I was very confident in sharing what my philosophy was. Looking back, however, when other coaches asked me about my views, often I noticed that my thoughts would shift here and there depending on the question or the day. I realize now my foundational philosophy was not concrete.

Even with legendary coach John Wooden's signed copy of his pyramid of success on my wall (this document defines Coach Wooden's coaching philosophy and is considered the mother of all coaching philosophies) — a document that I would refer to often — I hadn't put together what I was missing.

A side note here — I had the great honor to meet with John Wooden at his home in Encino, California in 2003. At that time, one of my players, Henry Meier (yes the same Henry Meier who edited this book), was dating a girl who's mother's sister was related to Coach Wooden. Are you following me?

Anyway, at our end of the season banquet, my team gave me as a gift a flight to LA to have lunch with John Wooden. To this day, it is one of the greatest gifts and coaching moments of my life. In 2003, I believe Coach Wooden was 93 or 94. Still unbelievably sharp, he shared some of his favorite poems with me (memorized), spoke of his love for his wife who had passed years before, and obviously talked a lot of basketball.

I had actually sent him a copy of my first book ahead of my visit, and he was going to jot down notes. Unfortunately, even though he made numerous comments, he couldn't find where he had left it. His home was literally wall-to-wall in books. How unbelievable would that have been? Coach Wooden writing comments on my book! Regardless, I did spend the next five hours with him and it's still one of my treasured memories.

One funny story from that experience was that after we returned from lunch from his favorite restaurant (he drove, by the way), he went over to his answering machine and checked his messages. Listening with him, one message went like this: "Hey coach, this is Bill and I'm just checking in on you. I heard that you've been out partying and going to the tattoo parlors with Dennis Rodman, and I just wanted to make sure you are doing ok." Coach Wooden looked at me and said "(Bill) Walton calls me everyday". Great stuff!

At the time I met Coach Wooden I was relatively comfortable with my coaching philosophy, but there was some flexibility to it and having views or statements that shifted a bit depending on who I spoke with always kind of bothered me.

One day I picked up a book written by Pete Carroll, the Hall of Fame football coach out of USC and now the head coach of the Seattle Seahawks. In the book, *Win Forever*, Carroll shared how he developed his personal philosophy. Reading it stopped me in my tracks. "That's it," I thought.

Carroll wrote about how he interviewed for jobs throughout his career, and described a scenario similar to mine, where, depending on the conversation, his philosophy would shift a bit regarding his belief system. Now here he is, by all accounts an incredibly successful coach, worrying about the same things I was.

Carroll's "aha!" moment came when he reread some of Coach Wooden's books and realized that it took Coach Wooden 16 years to fully develop his pyramid philosophy. In *Win Forever*, Carroll wrote:

> Wooden's real breakthrough came the moment he had developed his philosophy in a full, complete, and systematic way. It was only then that Wooden would go on to win 10 out of the next 12 national championships… The wealth of detail that went into Wooden's pyramid was incredible. He had figured out absolutely everything about his program — his belief system, his philosophy, his delivery, and a million other details that made his first championship possible. He had figured it out so completely that he could recreate it year after year after year. He had refined them to the point that he could explain them to the people around him.

In reading about Carroll's aha moment, it became mine, too.

Carroll knew what to do. He decided to develop his philosophy so he could be as clear in his mission as Wooden was to his. He then spent the next few months writing notes and filling binders. He said it was the sheer discipline of working at it that made it happen.

In reviewing his career and refining all of the elements that he knew were right for him, he ultimately created his own coaching pyramid that contained his overarching vision of what he wanted to stand for as a person, a coach, and a competitor. Everything he needed to win forever.

I knew I needed to do this as well. The time was now. Here I was in 2015, 29 years into my basketball coaching career, and I was going to wipe my slate clean and create my new foundation of coaching. Like Coach Carroll, I evaluated what I've done in the past. I graded myself in all areas and determined what I needed to do better, what things were still rock solid, and what new components I should add.

This process was invigorating. Over a two-month span, I created a document that contained my coaching life. It felt amazing. In this declaration were my 30 years of blood, sweat, and tears. I knew it forwards and backwards, and I felt supremely confident to share my vision with the world.

I truly believed I could interview for any head coaching position and that institution would be hard pressed to find someone more prepared. I still do.

The first team I presented my Waves Pyramid of Success to was my 2016 squad. It hadn't crossed my mind beforehand, but as I handed it out to my players for our beginning of the season meeting, I had a quick thought of, "What if they don't respond to this? This is my entire coaching life on one piece of paper. What if this falls flat?"

Fortunately, that image went out the window quickly. When I shared with them what each box meant or represented, I could see that they were buying in. We left that initial meeting totally united in our vision and I knew something special was about to happen.

That meeting paved the way for a spectacular season. We claimed our first conference title since 2012, made it all the way to the CIF Section final, advanced to the NorCals, and finished the year with a 23-6 record and a No. 8 ranking in the state.

I used this same pyramid the next three seasons and the meetings all went over similarly. And, by the way, so did our final results — that would be four league titles, four CIF Section Final Fours, two CIF Section title games, two NorCal appearances, one Norcal Final Four, and four top-eight rankings in the state, including one top-three finish. Over those four years we amassed a combined win loss record of 97-22. That averages out to more than 24 wins per season. Pretty impressive stuff.

Now winning, however, isn't the only way to measure the success of one's philosophy. But by every assessment, my foundational philosophy was working: my players were united; they played with a purpose and a fire that was tangible; they had fun, cared deeply about their sport and each other; and they represented their school with pride.

It's so fulfilling when you see the tears of joy, exuberance, and satisfaction at a banquet — and to hear your players and parents tell you how much their experience meant to them. What more do you want from a program?

I encourage you all to take stock of your career, life, health, or anything that's deeply important to you. By creating your own pyramid of success, you will certainly find more clarity, purpose, and fulfillment. Go after it!

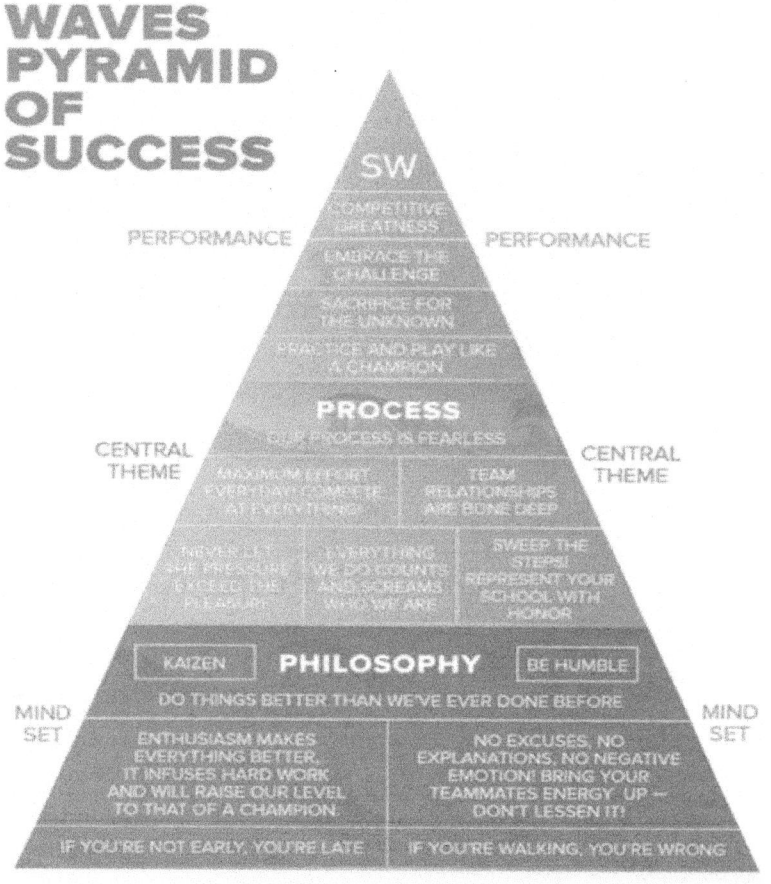

My Personal Coaching Philosophy

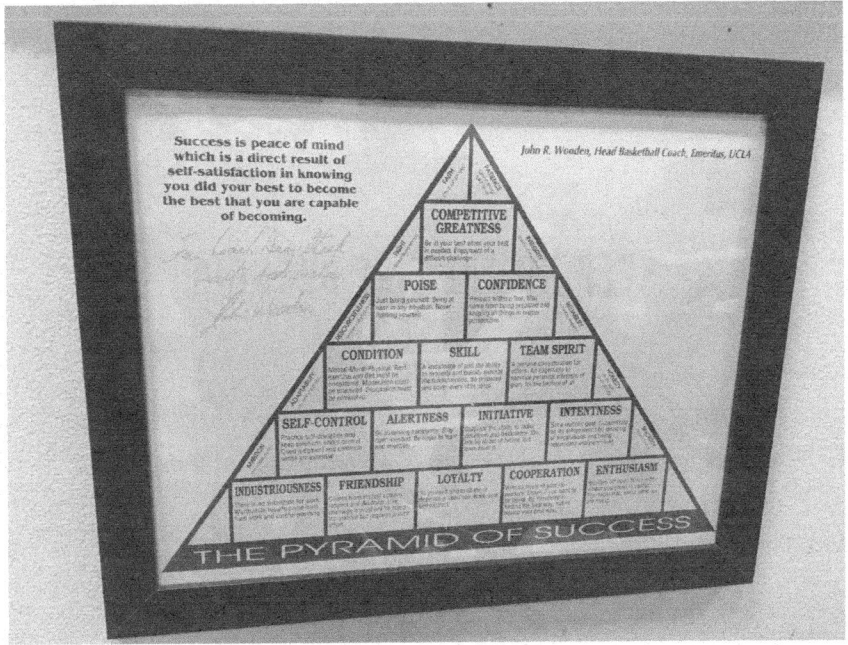

Coach Wooden's Pyramid of Success.

KEEPING THE FIRE BURNING

Passion sees no unstoppable barriers. It will plow through, jump across, or dig under any obstacles. Where some see a dead end, passion sees a possibility.

—Johnny M Hunt

Energy is essential to success. If there is no excitement, enthusiasm, or passion, there's no catalyst for achievement.

—David Cottrell

Coaches now have more access to information than in any other time in history. Whatever you need is a click away. Knowledge alone, however, is not enough to make a successful coach. Two coaches can have similar talent, run the same play and wind up with vastly different outcomes. The skill of coaching is not just aggregating knowledge, but putting that knowledge to work on a daily basis, and executing one's coaching philosophy consistently. It's still more art than science and can be difficult to teach. A good barometer for measuring success is how inspired players are by their coach.

In my last book, *A Waldorf Approach To Coaching Team Sports*, I spoke quite a bit on motivation and inspiration. The significance of it back in 2000 is equally important twenty years later. I still believe it's the biggest missing piece from most coaches' arsenals.

Being inspirational and motivating takes preparation, attention to detail, and finding ways to connect with players both individually and as a team. Just showing up to practice and jumping right into fundamentals is short-sighted. There's more to the game. But preparing to be inspiring is still not enough. A great coach also makes motivation a foundational part of who he or she is. It's personal.

In speaking to your players, you are telling a story. Do you want them attentive and waiting on every word that comes out of your mouth or staring back at you with glazed looks? This piece of the puzzle is huge.

In his book, *The Champion's Mind: How Great Athletes Think, Train, and Thrive*, Dr. Jim Afremow wrote of an experience that legendary University of North Carolina women's soccer coach Anson Dorrance once had. It was early morning, and Coach Dorrance was driving into work when off in the distance he saw one of his players doing extra training in the lonely hours. He later left a note at that player's locker that said: "The vision of a champion is someone who is bent over, drenched in sweat, at the point of exhaustion when no one else is watching."

The player whose locker he left the note on was Mia Ham, who would go on to achieve her goal of becoming the greatest player in the history of her sport.

As a coach, always be looking for ways to inspire. How impactful must it have been for Mia to return to her locker and read that note? I can almost promise you that she put that note in a place where she could read it daily, and that it continued to inspire her into the distant future. Use ideas like this and results will manifest.

In my first book, I shared many ways I have tried to inspire my teams over the years. I will share some of those again here.

Goal Setting

Every team needs to have clear, defined goals for what they want to accomplish. I believe the best setting for this is a team gathering at one of the players' homes, preferably the first or second week of the season. The timing is important because, if the team has had a few days together, they will begin forming a bond and will have some experience to draw on when thinking of ways to become better.

Setting goals is a part of most coaches' and teams' interactions. Every squad wants to be champions, but a coach plays a vital role in helping guide his or her team toward the right pursuits. He or she needs to ensure their players strive for the right things.

One of the worst things a coach can do is set only lofty or potentially unattainable goals. What happens to a team whose goals are to go undefeated and win the league championship if they lose a couple of games at the beginning of a season? The possibility of giving up or looking at their season as a disappointment is increased.

Our team goals may have those mentioned above, but they are way down the list. Make sure to include goals such as having fun, positivity, and unity.

Team Covenant

In the past, I have drawn up a team covenant with my players. This idea comes from one of the top coaches in the history of the game, Pat Riley.

A covenant is basically an agreement that binds people together. It comes from the entire team's input and everyone has to agree with it. When it's finished, everyone signs it and everyone gets a copy.

We came out of our first team meeting in '94 so fired up and so in tune with our mission for the season that nothing could have stopped us that year.

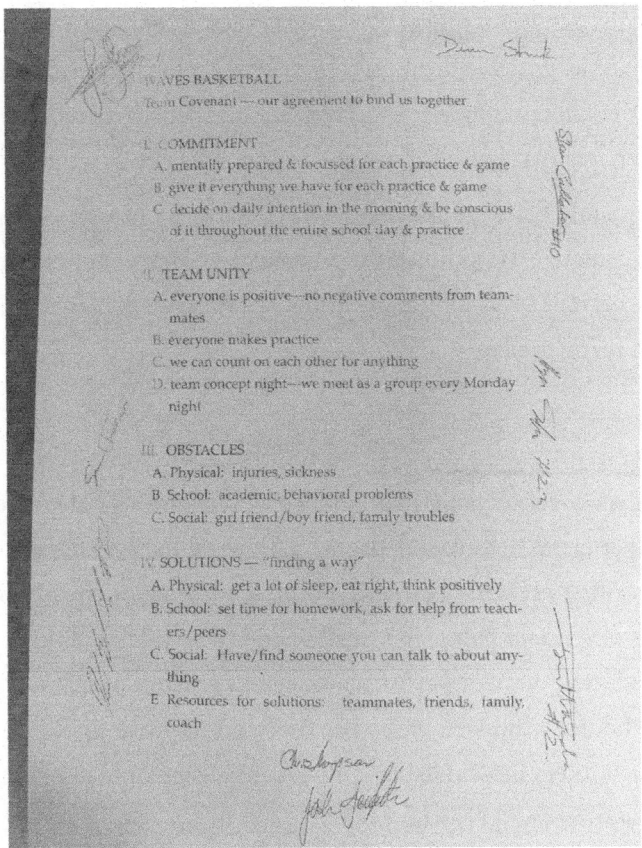

1994's Team Covenant.

Daily Intentions

Another positive way to motivate through goal setting is to have your players write out daily intentions. For years, my players have written down their individual and team goals for a season, signed them, and given them to me. This is a great ritual —- and my players continue to do this — but I have realized these goals don't live in some of the players on a daily basis.

With the daily intentions exercise, however, I have found that my players are much more conscious of their larger goals on a regular basis. At every practice, my players give me a signed list of intentions that they want to accomplish that day.

The list can be as short or as long as they want. A few examples are: going as hard as possible during every drill; showing no negative emotion; or being mentally prepared for today's practice. This is a great way to have your players ready themselves for upcoming practices or games.

I remember Andy Goncalves, who during my pregame talks during our playoff run in '91, would throw down a pad of paper at my feet with his intentions on it. He was letting me know — not so subtly! — that my point guard was ready to play.

Weekly Journal

One of the most-recent ideas I've come up with regarding player motivation is a weekly journal that players use to chart their individual performance. Where my other ideas are geared to pump up or prepare my players for an upcoming practice or game, the weekly journal is unique in that it enables them to reflect upon their performance after a practice or game is over and critique what they did well and what they can improve upon. My players found this tool very helpful in bringing greater insight into their connection with preparation and performance.

Weekly Improvement Journal   Week of: _____

QUESTIONS TO ASK YOURSELF:

Did I arrive mentally prepared?
Did I go as hard as I could?
Did I have a positive attitude?
What can I do better?

Sunday	Monday	Tuesday	Wednesday	Thursday	Friday	Saturday

Daily Quotes and Word Of Emphasis

A couple of years ago, I decided to add a word of emphasis and a daily quote as a focal point of practices, for example, enthusiasm. Then I found a quote that I felt properly defined the enthusiasm that I was looking for (for example: "Nothing great was ever achieved without enthusiasm" —Ralph Waldo Emerson). Don't underestimate this tool.

The day I realized I had something was with the first team I tried it with —- the 1993-94 squad. I had been doing it for a few weeks, and I thought it was going pretty well. On one particular day I was in the middle of saying, "And today's quote is by…" when suddenly the J.V. team practicing on the other end of the court started their lay-up drills with balls bouncing all over the place, making a lot of noise. In unison, my entire team turned around and yelled, "Hold the balls!" They wanted their quote to help motivate them for the start of practice.

Here are some ideas that I have added since the early 2000's. I hope you find a few that you want to try with your team.

In the past 10 years or so, I've tried to come up with a theme for the season. "Sacrifice for the unknown," "Do things better than you ever have done before," "Kaizen" (continuous improvement), and "be uncommon amongst the uncommon" are just a few of them. The last one was our theme for the 2020 season and the inspiration for the title of my book. When I shared this "be uncommon amongst the uncommon" quote with the team, I could tell it resonated. We even chanted a part of it after every practice or game. We would say "one, two, three, Waves, four, five, six, Uncommon". I believe when your team is reminded daily to be uncommon, it's more likely players will strive to be just that.

I got this quote from former Navy Seal and current motivational speaker David Goggins. You might want to check him out. He is intense and hardcore, but I love his tenacity.

My former star player, Chris Schwartz-Edmisten, shared with me how he loved that each year had a theme and how it helped to shape the season.

He even called me up when he was playing in college and asked what our theme was for each particular season. I truly believe this idea can help shape your season as well.

My teams still set goals. We've just amped it up. Every summer I hand write a personal letter to each of my players. I put a stamp on it, place it in the mailbox, and send it on its way. It's a little extra work to do it in this manner, but I believe there is something a bit more special in receiving a handwritten letter that arrives in an envelope in the mailbox.

Just the experience of opening it up and reading a message on an actual piece of paper that you can feel. It's a more special experience than reading a text or email.

It's also something that your players will reread more often and possibly even tape onto their walls. I know from experience — many of my players have told me they do just that. Some even tape it to their ceiling so it's the last thing they see before they close their eyes and go to sleep.

I also share with my players in the letter I send them my observations of their skill set, potential, and things they need to work on. I will also choose a personal quote for each of them — something that reminds me of them or their particular situation. This has also proven to be very powerful.

Next, I have them write down their goals of what they want to accomplish as a team, what they personally want to achieve, and how they are going to attain these goals. I want to hear their plan in detail.

I then choose a date where we will all meet. Sometimes it's been over the summer, and sometimes it's been in the fall after school has resumed. On this date, we meet early in the morning on a weekend at school. My wife, Aimee, and I have a rented van and are waiting for them. We then take a drive to a location Aimee and I have scoped out. They know to bring the letters (both mine and theirs), their running shoes, and water.

When we arrive at our destination, Aimee and I point to the mountain we are about to run up. We typically choose a route up that is about two to three miles long, mostly straight up, with somewhat challenging terrain;

the view from the top is always amazing. This run is usually about 25 to 35 minutes and it's very hard.

Remember, my guys are basketball players and not cross country athletes. I want to find something that is very challenging but doable. I want them to have a sense of accomplishment and feel like they achieved something as a team when finished. They always feel incredible when they reach the top and the first ones to finish always cheer on the rest.

When everyone reaches the top and is rested and hydrated, I have them take out both their letters and, one at a time, read them aloud. I can't emphasize enough how powerful this is. They have all just struggled mightily to run up a very steep mountain, all succeeded, and now are sharing their hopes, dreams, fears, potential, and shortcomings with their brothers, surrounded by panoramic beauty on top of the world. This activity is magical. I can't encourage you enough to try it with your team.

While planning and preparation are critical to motivating and inspiring a team, sometimes you have to be creative and find new methods on the fly.

Take the current situation we find ourselves in with the coronavirus: we are in the midst of a nationwide shutdown, no one is going to school, and everything is suddenly taking place online. My team can't meet, and I may not even see my guys until summer or later.

I realized that we needed to stay connected, so I sent a group text in March saying I would be sending them motivational words everyday until April 20 (our first scheduled day back at school). I also stated that if they hadn't heard from me by 5pm each evening that they needed to send me a reminder text. That was a way for them to take some ownership in the process — and also to gauge how important this exercise was to them.

So far, it's worked incredibly well. My players all enjoy the quotes and sending them through a group text brings about lively banter. My team remains united, and they are reminded daily to put in work. This exercise will definitely play a part in shaping our group. I can already see their commitment level ramping up.

In the future, I can see this evolving into video presentations of what each player is doing to push his limits as well. As creative as Waldorf students are, I'm sure we have only scratched the surface on how we will face this obstacle in front of us. So far, the coronavirus is not keeping us down.

When we reach April 20, I will then ask them to take turns, rotating one by one, offering an inspirational quote or thought day by day that they chose. Everyone does their part.

As a coach, you always have to have the pulse of your team. I'm certain there are a lot of programs out there right now that are missing a golden opportunity to deepen their connection. Not the Waves!

Different finishing destinations from our team runs

LEADING BY EXAMPLE

The most powerful leadership tool you have is your own personal example.

—-John Wooden

Motivating and inspiring a group of young men or women is an intimate experience, and part of that intimacy is staying true to one's convictions. If a coach is preaching about discipline and commitment and they can't take care of their own life, the message will fall on deaf ears. There are too many coaches out there that are in terrible shape, have horrible diets, and as a result are a poor role model for their players.

A coach has such a great opportunity to lead by example in this regard. I don't know how a coach can be motivational (in terms of demanding that his team work hard, condition, and be disciplined) when it's clear that it's nonexistent in his or her own world.

I personally take great pride in my health, and my players know that I train hard daily. There are even coaches out there that call me the Jack LaLanne of coaches. I don't know if it's true or not, but the bottom line is my players know that I'm not asking them to do things I can't or won't do myself, and that I stand behind my word. By living and coaching this way, it lends you credibility in the eyes of your players.

It's important to understand the conviction presented in your message. Again, this goes back to how one takes care of themselves. If one is fit and committed to a healthy lifestyle, the odds are strongly in your favor that you will have greater energy and enthusiasm when you are sharing your daily focal points. This element can have a great impact on your players. Conversely, your players will also know if you are faking it.

Four years ago, I read a story about Kyle Korver, the longtime NBA player. He is considered one of the greatest three-point shooters in NBA history. The story was about what Kyle would do to motivate himself in the offseason.

Through a friend, Kyle had heard about an ancient japanese purification ritual called Misogi. There are multiple translations of the word that have evolved over the years, but it's recently been more connected to a feat of athletic endurance. The goal of the Misogi is to choose some activity to be completed in one day that is so difficult that you aren't sure if it's possible to accomplish.

Korver jumped at this idea.

He and his friend got together and came up with a plan —- they were going to get in a boat with an 80 pound rock, and weighted vests. They would row out in the ocean and drop the rock to the bottom — about 10 feet down. From there it gets a little crazy. While one of them was treading water, the other would dive down to the ocean floor, pick up the 80 pound rock and start running underwater while holding his breath. When their lungs felt like they were going to explode, the one running would drop the rock, come to the surface, catch his breath and start treading water. The other would now take his turn diving to the bottom, picking up the rock and continuing the run where the other had stopped. The two of them did this for four and a half hours —- the time it took to complete five kilometers (3.1 miles). What an unbelievable accomplishment!

Reading about this feat blew my mind, and I started thinking, "What could I do?" And then I had the thought, "What could my team do?" The more I pondered it, the more excited I was. Instead of choosing a one-day event, I thought it might be more impactful if we expanded the idea and made it a long-term competition.

I have continued this tradition almost every year. My first personal Misogi took place in 2017 and my goal was to cycle (road bike) 4,000 miles in 20 weeks. I was a 20 miles, two to three times a week cyclist when I took on this challenge. The thought of riding 200 miles a week for 20 weeks seemed almost impossible. That's the beauty of it: I didn't know if I could do it. To this day, it's probably the hardest thing I've done athletically. I was able to accomplish it because I told my players that I was going to do it and I couldn't let them down.

In the ensuing years, I have come up with Misogi challenges for the team and myself. As I am writing this, I have challenged my players to complete 4,332 workout sessions between April 20 and September 6 — a period of 140 days. With 13 players involved that averages out to 333 workout sessions per player, which is undoubtedly an incredibly challenging figure. In my mind, three workouts a day is the goal. If they can complete this challenge successfully, however, it will speak volumes to their commitment and focus going into the next season.

I've also shared with them my current Misogi — one that will push me to my limit as well. Yes, coaches, you will have to walk your talk, but it's a great opportunity to forge a deeper bond with your team, and do some wonderful things for yourself as well.

Pushing limits: that, for me, has been an integral part to finding personal strength as well as motivating my teams. Finding a way to exceed what already seems daunting opens up worlds of possibility.

One of my favorite anecdotes that exemplifies hard work and the heart of a champion is a story I've shared with my guys about Lance Armstrong, arguably the greatest cyclist of all time. Say what you want about his ethics, but there is no denying that Lance was a beast.

Here's the story: Armstrong is training for the Tour De France, and on this particular day he was hill training. His goal was to understand better the nuances of the climb up a particular mountain so he would be fully prepared when he climbed it for real in the race. He had already ridden for two-plus hours just to reach the base of the climb.

The weather was awful — snow, sleet, and wind peppered him as he pedaled on. The steep hillside climb would be a 60-minute ride, virtually straight up. With his coach following him in a car, Armstrong battled the elements and made his trek up the mountain. More than an hour passed before Lance finally reached the top. His coach pulled up alongside him and said, "OK good. Get in the car and have some hot tea." Lance hesitated, though, and said he was unhappy about the way he had ridden. He said he didn't fully understand the climb, that he was still uncertain about how to pace himself up. The coach responds, "What's the problem? You got it, let's go." Lance just shakes his head and says, "No, I have to go back and do it again." DO IT AGAIN!!!!!!!

Are you kidding me? He rode over two hours just to get to the base of the mountain, pedaled straight uphill for another hour in snow and sleet, got to the top but still wasn't satisfied.

I believe he is the only person on the planet that would be willing to go through that level of pain. He put in seven hours on his bike in hellish conditions just so he would have an advantage when he was on that hill for the race.

Armstrong believed that he was the best because he knew he was willing to suffer more than any other person alive. I bring up stories like that when I'm challenging my guys. Players need strong examples of what is possible.

A coaches' health, energy, and activity level is an important guiding light in motivating a team because, I believe, no one can be the coach they want to be without vibrant health. It overrides all aspects of your personality and performance.

Take it from me. I have overcome four knee surgeries, back surgery, and degenerative discs in my neck and back. I've spent three years on and off in tremendous pain due to a back condition. It absolutely affected my mood, performance, marriage, and enjoyment of life. For seven months I couldn't sit or tie my shoes. Do you know how depressing it is to have someone tie your shoes everyday?

There were times when I was scared. I asked myself, "Is this going to be the rest of my life?" I kept waiting for improvement that never came. My saving grace, though, was that I could always see myself getting better and I was never going to give up. And if there was another option, I was going to pursue it.

I know there are a lot of people out there that have chronic pain issues. I realize everyone is different, but I want to share with you what ultimately helped me.

I got a lot of help and emotional comfort from a wonderful upper cervical chiropractor named Dr. Desiree Crusade that started me on the right track. I still see her to this day. She was supremely confident that I was going to get better, and I believe her positivity seeped into my being.

I also read books titled *The Mindbody Prescription* by John Sarno, *The Meaning of Truth* by Nicole Sachs, and *Can't Hurt Me* by David Goggins. All of these books ask you to put in work to help yourself. This was pivotal for me because I had always felt in the back of my mind that I would play a big part in my healing.

For a long time I would go to one practitioner after another in hopes that he or she would heal me, and never get the results that I wanted. Taking control of my own healing really gave me the tools I needed to start down my path to health and well being.

Finally, I got a name from Goggins book that gave me the missing piece to my puzzle. Goggins body was battered by three tours of Navy Seal training and years of ultra marathon races and pushing his body to the limits.

He wrote that his body was locked up, nothing was helping and he truly felt that he was going to live out the rest of his days in pain. He remembered, however, that there was a guy on the Seal base that was an expert in stretching and advanced mental training methods and that he had invented a stretching protocol that had changed many lives for the better. Goggins started to think that maybe — just maybe! — this regimen could help him.

I, too, was in a place where my body was locked up. I knew I needed greater flexibility, but every time I tried to stretch it seemed like I got worse. With Dr. Crusade's help and the knowledge and work I put in from the other books, I felt like I might be ready to try to stretch again. And now I might know of someone that can show me how to do it safely.

His name is Joe Hippensteel. I Googled his website and sent out an email. To my surprise, Joe himself called me back personally and told me that he had Googled me as well. He knew that I was a coach, teacher, athletic director, and that I had written a book. That impressed me. I shared with him my situation and he actually put me through a stretching routine during that very phone call. Talk about "Uncommon."

It turned out that he was offering a workshop in San Diego in a week and a half and he told me I needed to be there. I do believe that some things are just meant to be and I felt the timing of this was just too perfect to pass up. I jumped on a plane 10 days later and spent four full days learning how to stretch for my body.

I stretched for four to five hours a day and learned how to help others stretch for four to five hours as well. My body was a mess but I actually felt a little improvement by the end of the workshop. I took what I learned home with me and I have been stretching everyday since. At this point I have been stretching daily since November 15, 2019. That is 126 consecutive days (after I stretch this evening) and counting. My first 100 days I spent a minimum of 40 minutes per day. Now I do at least 30.

With no intention of stopping and knowing that stretching is part of my Misogi for the spring and summer, I expect my number will hit 297 on September 6. Beast mode!

And that's just too close to a full year to stop there. Habits are a beautiful thing.

I share this journey through healing — and some of my physical exploits — because my health and fitness level has been vital to my success throughout my career. When healthy, it's given me confidence, energy, and a level of trust from my players that knowledge and expertise alone can't bring.

My players feed off my passion, energy and yes, physical prowess. I kid you not that just 20 minutes ago I got off the phone with one of my players, Sam Bosque, and we were marveling at the fact that we both reeled off 400 push ups today without knowing about the other's intention to do so. He is inspired with regard to our upcoming Misogi in April and he is trying to implement a mini Misogi from now until then to keep his teammates active through this world crisis.

These are some of the things that can happen when a coach is leading the way.

Battling one's health is also a powerful teacher. All of my players witnessed the pain I went through in recent years. They also saw that I never missed a day and never complained. They knew I was committed to getting better and was going to do whatever it took to make it happen.

I would be foolish to think that I am out of the woods. I know there will be many more obstacles to come. But I also know that I have a lot of tools in my shed to combat what comes my way and an open mindset to live my life vibrantly.

THE CHALLENGES IN WINNING

If one advances confidently in the direction of his dreams, and endeavors to live the life, which he has imagined, he will meet with a success unexpected in common hours.

—Henry David Thoreau

I believe in preparation. I believe in attention to detail. There is nothing magical about winning. It's the same with every team - preparation and attention to detail.

—Sean Payton

The importance of winning in sports can be a very controversial topic, especially at a Waldorf school. As a coach, your philosophy of winning needs to be clearly defined. From expectations for practice, offseason commitments, and playing time in games, a coach has to be able to speak with conviction in regard to how big a part winning plays in the ultimate goal of a team's experience.

I was raised in an extremely competitive environment and played at top-level high school sports and college baseball programs where winning was imperative. It's fair to say that it fueled my motivation. I craved it.

Career ending knee surgeries during my college years, however, started to slowly transform my perception of what is truly important in sports.

When I started at Sacramento Waldorf in 1984 as the baseball coach, I learned very early that my views on sports and the school's views differed. Stepping onto the campus was actually a bit of a culture shock: the baseball field was just a patch of grass — with no pitchers mound, backstop or dugouts — and Beverly, the school's cow, grazed near second base.

In my first meeting with the team, I only had a few players that had any organized (Little League) experience. My best player said he hadn't played in a real game, but he had read a lot of books about it. Alrighty then…

In my early interactions with the high school faculty, they stated that the sports teams would practice twice a week and that the goal for their sports program was to win 50 percent of its games. I was floored. I countered that the teams had to practice five times a week and if their students get a 50 percent on their tests, they fail. Point scored. They didn't have a response for that one.

In time, however, I realized where they were coming from. Sac Waldorf had never really had a sports program and this was a big step for the school. There were also huge concerns with regard to competition, and a fear that the importance of sports would outgrow other pursuits within the student body and undermine the goal of producing well-rounded individuals.

We ultimately agreed that teams would practice four days a week and to strive to do as well as we could in games and matches. The faculty supported their new sports program, but was still taking a wait-and-see attitude as to how it would go.

I entered Sac Waldorf at a very opportune time. We were joining a league and beginning to participate in multiple sports. But what did I get myself into? I was used to top-flight facilities and athletes that were talented and competitive. Now I have a cow on the field and a bunch of book readers for a team.

I'm happy to say it's all turned out pretty well. The community embraced our sports program and, in many ways, the Friday night basketball games are what brings everyone together more than anything else. It is absolutely woven into the fabric of our culture.

I, too, found greater balance in my relationship with sports and started to appreciate the finer points of what competition could bring.

As a young boy and throughout high school and college, my view of winning was similar to that of the legendary football coach Vince Lombardi, who once said, "Winning isn't everything, it's the only thing." In fact, I had a childhood friend who often joked that I must have gone to the (fictitious) "Vince Lombardi School of Intensity" because I played as if everything was life and death.

As I have matured and gained experience leading high school athletes, I am now closer to former tennis champion Jimmy Connors who quipped, "I think my greatest victory was every time I walked out there, I gave it everything I had. I left everything out there. That's what I'm most proud of."

Just know that as a coach, you play a huge role in how your team will view victory and defeat. It's ok to hold your team accountable, carry high expectations, and strive to be the best you can possibly be. But don't ever forget to celebrate your team's effort, unity, and commitment. Those characteristics will always be the true mark of a winner.

Let me give you an example. In 1991, my team may have achieved our program's greatest victory with a win over a powerhouse Ponderosa team in their own tournament. They were ranked 3rd in all of Sacramento at the time. The following year we almost knocked them off again and I know their outstanding veteran coach, Terry Battenberg, wasn't too happy about it.

My '93 squad was solid but not to the level of my past couple teams. We were traveling to play Ponderosa again and I could sense that Coach Battenberg's team was ready. He had his typical dominant team and they were intent on crushing us. They full court pressed us the entire game and left their starters in till the end. They did everything possible to break our spirit, but we weren't having it.

My guys battled all night and never once backed down to the challenge. Even though we lost by 17, Pondo couldn't make us quit. We left everything on that court. As I entered their freezing cold locker room after the game, senior center Kai Schneider was lying across a row of mini-lockers — totally exhausted — with steam billowing up from his shaved head. That image has stayed with me my entire career. It was such a special moment epitomizing what sports can be and mean — and it had very little to do with the final score.

In these moments, a coach needs to honor and appreciate the traits his or her team exemplifies on the court. Take the time to acknowledge effort, toughness, and resolve. The scoreboard said that we got smoked that night, but I couldn't have been more proud.

Back to the struggle that winning can be.

Almost right out of the gate, my teams won early and often. We had great success in baseball and basketball. It got to the point after our '91 teams both went undefeated in league, I felt like this was how it's always going to be. I had been there for eight years and we had five league titles in baseball, and in the six seasons of coaching basketball, we had claimed four. And both sports were riding four-year conference championship streaks. Life was good.

Looking back on it, I seldom spoke to my team about winning. We were all about practicing the right way, respecting the sport and our opponent, and doing everything we could to deserve our success.

What I didn't realize at the time, is that a coach doesn't define his or her philosophy when they are always winning. It's much easier to not talk about it or stress it to your players when one is always successful.

We kept that streak alive through '92, but things started changing for us in the middle of the decade. I could see the writing on the wall and it was also becoming a challenge for me to coach both sports. In '95, we had nine seniors on our baseball team and I wanted to see them through. I also knew that this was going to be it for me. As great of a group as they were, and even enjoying another championship season with them, I knew my time with baseball was over. It was time to focus solely on hoops.

In basketball, however, 1995 would start a string of eight years where we would only win one league title. It was this period where I really started to define who I was as a coach and where my philosophy on winning would crystalize.

This is where striving to succeed, dedication, sacrifice, and heart became more than just nice words to say. If my team exemplified those traits, they were winners. We would still be disappointed with a game loss, but there was solace in knowing that we did everything in our power to succeed.

Let me be clear —- there is nothing wrong with winning. Everyone wants to win. Where the calculation gets murky is figuring out how to foster a winning mentality without creating an environment where players burn out.

Everywhere I look, programs have a year-round mentality. My brother, Terry, is an extraordinarily successful high school football coach in the Sacramento area. His teams make a habit of winning league titles and making deep runs in the playoffs every season. Often his squad ends it's year in early December only to start weight training on Jan. 1 in preparation for the next season. There is almost no downtime. That's what strong teams do.

Today, in order to keep up with the Joneses, basketball programs are participating in (after the school season ends) Spring, Summer, and Fall leagues. They are also doing mandatory weight training, attending team camps, and practicing whenever it's legal to do so.

I can still remember one frustrated father, who had his high school freshman son playing in a powerhouse program at a prestigious school, share with me that his boy had practice six days a week, mandatory weight training, and film study — for a 9th grade program.

That's too much...and his son quit basketball before his junior year. At some point, there needs to be a voice of reason. Honestly, there are very few athletes that are so dedicated that a year round commitment appeals to them. They just endure it until they can't.

Having said that, however, I am all for athletes working out year round — if it's their choice. I love inspiring my players with quotes or stories of professional athletes who are putting in work to chase their dreams. In turn, it's a joy to see my guys commit to their sport by doing individual offseason programs. This is so powerful for me because it's coming from them. These aren't mandatory team training sessions, and no one is penalized for not pursuing a program. It's internal and I believe a more valuable experience for them to navigate.

I also love to see athletes crosstrain in different sports. That's one of the special qualities of our school. Student athletes have an opportunity to participate in any sport they are interested in. That's also a part of why our teams don't do more formal offseason training —- so athletes don't have to choose between two sports. Our voice of reason is balance.

Remember, though, I do want to win, and I believe striving to win is incredibly important. There are many wonderful habits one can develop in this pursuit. A piece of it, however, has to be individual. If there is a player that has aspirations to be a Division I college player, and that is his or her dream, one should never stand in their way.

I actually have one of those such players that might be coming to play at Sac Waldorf this next season. He is a young man named Trevor Button, and he is planning on transferring from a Waldorf school in North Carolina to attend Sacramento Waldorf. He is a bonafide D1 college prospect and has past roots in this area. His current school will not field a team next year, and he wants to continue playing to chase his dream.

To say I'm excited to work with him is an understatement. From what I know of him, he's an incredibly committed and hard working young man that can never get enough. He is one of those rare athletes that would thrive in any year-round program. He is the exception.

For athletes at Sac Waldorf, we only require that they commit to their season of sport. We expect them to make practice daily, and give it their best. The offseason is up to them and how they want to fill it. Again, it doesn't mean they can't do more, but it's just their choice. We put it in their hands. This is an important distinction.

It's equally important to recognize what comes with that choice. Shutting one's sport down the day it ends and not picking it up again until the following season brings about its own set of challenges. In doing this, you are absolutely limiting your potential for improvement. That, in turn, will put you farther behind your teammates that are committing to their sport and will potentially affect your playing time and possibly even your enjoyment as well.

Those are real consequences. On the other side of the coin, sacrificing your social life or putting all your eggs in one basket to attack your dream has risks also. It's possible that one could put everything they have into that one goal and fall short. All of those eggs were put into training the entire summer to earn a starting spot and one still ended up on the bench? Then what? Well, the late great Kobe Bryant said, "You better get yourself more eggs." Meaning, set another goal. That's the winner's mindset. Yes, the possibility of viewing oneself in a negative light exists, but that can't stop you.

There are risks in striving, but what in life doesn't come with such risk? Playing it safe doesn't serve you. As Nelson Mandella said, "Your playing small doesn't serve the world. Who are you not to be great?"

Winning does come at a price. I ask my players often, "Do you deserve your success?"

At its best, the striving to win mentality is a blueprint for hard work, time management, goal setting, handling failure, and learning what it truly takes to be special. Seeing all your hard work lead to great results can be a recipe for your future successes.

Yes, playing it safe and not testing your limits may give you an excuse as to why you didn't achieve your goals. It may also give you more free time to hang out with your friends, but I can almost guarantee you when you look back at your choices, they will be viewed with disappointment.

One of my favorite quotes really speaks to this — "The pain of discipline is far less than the pain of regret."

YOU MUST GET BETTER

Today I will do what others won't do, so tomorrow I can accomplish what others can't.

—Jerry Rice

There's no talent here. This is hard work. This is an obsession. Talent does not exist, we are all human beings. You could be anyone if you put in the time. You will reach the top, and that's that. I am not talented. I am obsessed.

—Conor McGregor

The heights by great men reached and kept
Were not attained by sudden flight,
But they, while their companions slept,
Were toiling upward in the night

—Henry Wadsworth Longfellow

When I've been asked over the years how I've been able to coach for as long as I have, my response has always hovered around the desire to improve. Add my thirst for learning and a need to give my players a special experience, and you have a recipe for interest that is always with me.

Throughout my career, I have followed a number of high profile coaches — John Wooden, Dean Smith, Rick Pitino, Tom Izzo, Bobby Knight, Mike Kryzewski at the college level; and Pat Riley, Gregg Popovich, Brad Stevens, and Steve Kerr at the professional level. Always looking for a nugget that would help my team, listening to the greatest in my field speak about their craft is a perfect place to acquire knowledge. Sometimes, it's something as simple as a quote that inspires me to create a special experience for my team or to amp up my motivation for a season. I don't just limit myself to basketball coaches, I follow other top coaches in all sports in hope of gaining an edge.

Before I delve into improving one's craft, I have to share a story about an experience my wife, Aimee, and I had this past summer. In a weird way, it is related to striving to improve.

Aimee and I went to Las Vegas this past August for some rest and relaxation. We don't gamble, but she's always wanted to go to Chef Gordan Ramsey's Hell's Kitchen restaurant, and we like to people-watch, walk, and take in the sights.

It turned out, however, that the USA Men's Olympic Developmental Basketball team happened to be training in Vegas at the same time and we were all staying in the same hotel. Talk about fortunate timing! Every evening we would pass by the likes of Donovan Mitchell, Anthony Davis, Jayson Tatum, Kemba Walker, and De'Aaron Fox. I'm not usually star struck, but I have to say it was pretty cool.

But that was only the beginning. As Aimee and I are walking along in the Wynn casino, Golden State Warriors head coach Steve Kerr walked right past us. A couple minutes later Boston Celtics head coach Brad Stevens passed by as well. Now that was big! As I mentioned, those are two of my favorite NBA coaches.

At the top of my list, however, is Gregg Popovich, the San Antonio Spur's head coach and the head coach of the Olympic team. Would we possibly see him too? We kept our eyes peeled, but he never appeared.

The next morning we got up early and hit the gym. We wanted to get our training session out of the way, and start our day. In the gym, there were a couple of USA players lifting, but I didn't recognize them. At one point, though, I looked over at the cardio machines and I saw this older gentleman walking on the treadmill. It couldn't be, could it? I walked a little closer and…yes it was — Gregg Popovich. Now, it's on. I have to meet him. I may never get this opportunity again.

I've already met the greatest college coach ever in John Wooden and now I want to meet arguably the greatest NBA coach. At that time, an idea hit me. When I spent time with Coach Wooden, I asked him if he would diagram his favorite out of bounds play for me. He did, signed it, and I proudly display it on top of my desk in my office. Could I possibly get Coach Pop to do the same?

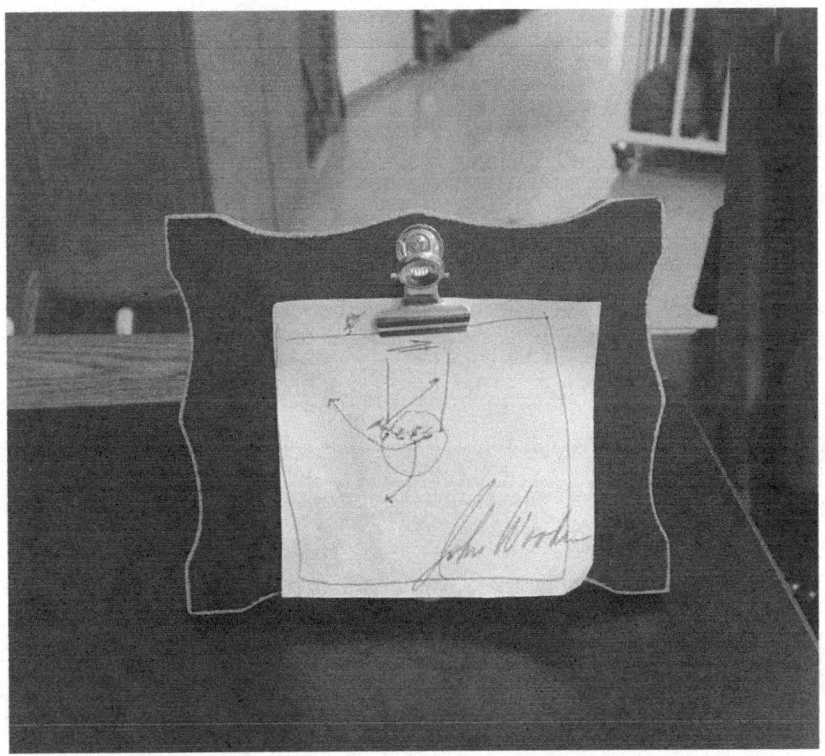

Coach Wooden's favorite baseline out of bounds play

With nothing to write with, I send Aimee sprinting back to our room to find a pen and paper. I'm keeping a watchout. As Aimee exited the elevator, she walked right into Coach K — Mike Kryzewski. What was happening? Another Hall of Famer!

Unfortunately, though, as I continued my lookout and prepared to stop Pop as he left the gym, he actually took an alternate route and walked out an internal exit that I wasn't aware of and disappeared down another hallway. Coach Pop was gone. Dang!

For the rest of our trip we were on the prowl to meet him but never saw him again. It did, however, give me the idea of trying to get an out of bounds play from my Mount Rushmore of NBA coaches — Popovich, Riley, Stevens, and Kerr. I've since written letters to all of them, and now I'm just hoping for a response. Cant hit a home run if you don't come to bat, right?

And who knows, if one or more of them do write back, it will be a shining example of reaching out to the experts to add to your knowledge. You never know when opportunity will knock.

Ok, back to getting better.

In searching for ways to improve, an idea from legendary former North Carolina Head Coach Dean Smith always has stayed with me. He said early in his career he committed an entire summer each year to study in depth one aspect of the game. Now realize that there are many parts to the basketball puzzle, but conquering one per year will make you a master if you stay at it long enough.

For me, this summer is going to be all about rebounding, rebounding, rebounding. I even bought shirts for my team (which I haven't given out yet) that say, NO REBOUNDS NO TITLES on the front.

Another powerful idea on how to hone your skills is a gem that I got from reading Rick Pitino's book *The One Day Contract*. The premise of this book is to treat each day as if your employer will evaluate your performance for that shift. And based on that evaluation, will decide if you will be rehired for the following day. Could you imagine?

The brilliance of this mindset is it really encourages you to prepare, be efficient, make the most of each day, live in the present, and to feel the power of making a contract with yourself. Pitino wrote, "Ask yourself this question: Whatever your job is, whatever you're working at right now, how would life be different if you were on a one day contract? How might your approach change if this afternoon after you finished work, a supervisor would make the call on whether to retain you for another day or let you go?"

To give you a little more of Coach Pitino's process, he said in order to benefit from a one day contract mentality, you need to make three promises to yourself: you will not quit, you will not procrastinate, and you will not allow discouragement to sideline you.

From there, you must prepare the night before — plan out your strategy for the next day. Pitino writes, "This is more than a to do list. It is a mindset that you train yourself to develop." He adds, "And when crafting your one day contract, you will want to think about not only what tasks you want to complete or actions you want to take, but about what mindset you want to instill, and what you are building toward in your day's work. And finally, there's the element of evaluation. Did you complete the tasks?"

If you are anything like me, sticking with this one day contract mindset for an extended time frame will be challenging. It takes great discipline. I certainly haven't used it consistently, mostly here and there.

However, a few years ago when our school administration was making sweeping changes and a lot of employees were on high alert, this strategy gave me great confidence. Everyone was being evaluated, but instead of freaking out and hoping I would survive the cuts, I just implemented Pitino's strategy and it helped insure me to be at the top of my game everyday. Following these principles, I promise you your productivity will skyrocket.

We live in an age where information is everywhere. It's literally at your fingertips. You have the resources to tap into any aspect of your area of interest. Take advantage of this. Make a plan. Determine what you need to work on and follow through.

As important as knowledge is, however, don't sleep on the presentation. Remember, there is a world of difference in how Gregg Popovich and a middle school coach would teach the same play. Seek out experts that you can talk to, visit, or better yet, have them attend your practice.

These past two years I had one of the finest high school basketball coaches in town, Drew Hibbs, stop by my practice to work with my team. He was a two time state champion coach who was taking time off from coaching to raise his children. It's enlightening to see how the best in their field work, and it's also fantastic for your players to experience a different voice. I can't encourage you enough to seek out greatness.

Another part of one's Kaizen (continuous improvement), is an expectation that what you are going to give to your team is important.

Many years ago, I read a book by Lou Holtz, the retired Hall Of Fame Notre Dame football coach. In *Winning Every Day*, Holtz shared a story about how he and another coach were talking about expectations. At this time, Holtz was the head coach at North Carolina State. Holtz wrote, "As we talked he asked me, 'Lou, are you the best football coach in the country?' Since Woody Hayes, Bear Bryant and 100 other fine coaches were still walking the planet I had to answer truthfully. 'No,' I replied, 'but I want to be.' (Lou's) friend said, 'Well, then you are stealing NC State's money and you should resign. They hired you because they thought you are the best coach in the country for that job. For you to say anything less is a disservice to your employer.'"

That comment has always resonated with me. No, Sac Waldorf didn't hire me to be the best basketball coach in the country. They just wanted me to start the program and give the student athletes a healthy, rich experience. But what I've realized through the years is I have an extraordinary opportunity to impact my players not just for a particular season but for the rest of their lives. I owe it to my school and players to strive for greatness.

The lessons a coach instills can help shape and mold his or her players futures. What is more gratifying and important than that? And yes, I do want to be the best coach in the country. It doesn't matter that I'm not. I realize that I'm not coaching the Lakers or the Olympic team.

However, I am content in knowing that I'm doing everything I can to get better, that I'm honoring my school with my efforts, and serving my players to the best of my ability.

And who knows, maybe the Lakers will call next year. :)

A COACH'S LIST

A coach will impact more young people in a year than the average person does in a lifetime.

—Billy Graham

In my previous book, there was a section that covered a lot of the areas that a coach must be prepared for. I've received so many calls over the years inquiring about different aspects of coaching that I felt like I should revisit this topic and update some of the strategies that I use to get ready for a season.

Knowledge and Expertise

It goes without saying that every solid coach has a thorough grasp of basic fundamentals, and a complete understanding of his or her own playbook. Entering a season, coaches should be prepared to teach with confidence in all areas that will be an emphasis on his or her team's blueprint.

Beyond the day to day skill building, I want to also have a specific focus (based on my current team's strengths and weaknesses) that I call my "Areas of Excellence." In this domain, I typically choose four or five areas that I want my team to be special in. Examples would be: half-court defense, team chemistry, limiting turnovers, or half court offensive execution. Breaking the year down into smaller components helps my teams stay more locked in to our yearly goals. My personal mantra is I want my team to be "Brilliant in the Basics.'"

Planning

Each season, based on my personnel, I have a general idea of how I want our year to unfold. I have certain things that we need to focus on by the time we play our first preseason game and certain things that don't need to be implemented until closer to the start of our league schedule. For example, during the early part of the season, we work mostly on our man-to-man defense and our continuity-type offenses. These are the staples of what we do.

It's also important to note that plans can change. A good coach has to have an open mind and be able to pivot and move in a different direction if his or her team's skill strengths are dictating it. This happened to me just this past year with my 2020 team.

Going into the season, I was 100 percent sure that we were going to be a full court pressing and fast breaking team. This was the shortest group I had ever coached (not one player taller than six foot), we had no low post presence, and I just didn't think we would be able to defend at a high enough level in the half court. I felt like we had to speed up the game in order to compete.

A month into our season, however, we were showing signs of being better in our half court defense than in our full, and our execution offensively in the half court was better than anticipated as well. I actually scrapped our full court defense and toned down our transition, something I never thought I would do with this squad. From that point on, we were a much better team.

Back to planning.

Cover the basics first and as you get closer to your league season, start adding quick hitters, trapping defenses, and special situation plays. Another advantage of approaching your season in this way is that other coaches who scout your team in the preseason will not have seen your entire system. Your players, too, will appreciate not being overloaded with too many things to learn all at once.

Practice

Practice is the key to the success of your team and my favorite part of coaching. Very seldom, if ever, are you going to to coach a team so talented that you don't need to practice soundly to win. John Wooden, in his book *They Call Me Coach* wrote, "More than likely any league championship or post-season success will be a result of the quality work done on the practice floor."

Remember, we only practice four days a week at Sac Waldorf so I need to make sure that the time my players spend is very well used.

I come prepared for each practice. I need to be able to demonstrate each drill, play, and fundamental with skill, enthusiasm and confidence. Second, I teach drills of a short duration. Our drills last typically anywhere from one to four minutes. It's important to keep things moving briskly. It's also important to have the right person demonstrating the drills.

Make sure the person (player or coach) knows how to do them properly. You don't want someone teaching the wrong form. Also, don't spend too much time explaining a drill or play. Players' bodies can get tight and any momentum that has been built up can crash and burn. What works for me is to demonstrate, have a short explanation, and then practice it.

Another helpful hint is to alternate difficult (physically taxing) drills with less challenging drills. For example, I want to do shooting drills right after a full court defensive or conditioning drill. This creates a game-like situation for shooting because my players are fatigued and breathing hard. Shooting one-and-one free throws is also a good drill to do after your team is winded.

One final thought for structuring practice: how to end it. Coach Wooden said he always tried to finish practice on a positive note. I totally agree. It's probably the last thing your players are going to remember and you want them to go home happy and excited about coming back the next day. Take advantage of this time by complimenting their effort and pointing out their improvement.

TYPICAL DAILY PRACTICE PLAN

5 min - Talk - Focus Of The Day - attention to detail,

Quote to emphasize our focus - "It's the little details that are vital. Little things make big things happen." - John Wooden

4 min - Layups

DEFENSIVE BREAKDOWN DRILLS

3 min - Positive pivots/ close-outs

3 min - Mirror drill

4 min - Help and recover

6 min - Defending screens

8 min - Shell drill

1 min - 1 and 1 free throw

TRANSITION DRILLS

4 min - Sprint dribble layups (full court)

4 min - Pitch ahead (full court)

5 min - 5-0 patterned fast break (full court)

3 min - Florida transition drill (full court)

1 min - 1 and 1 free throw

SHOOTING DRILLS

5 min - Triple Threats, attacking the basket

5 min - Post Moves

4 min - 20/20 (3 pt drill)

4 min - Larry Bird (3 pt drill)

3 min - 5 spots/5 shots

1 min - 1 and 1 free throw

1 min - Skip passes

6 min - Zone offense 5-0

10 min - Zone offense 5-5

8 min - Man offense 5-0

12 min - Man offense 5-5

5 min - Extra Conditioning

5 min - Free Throws

Pregame Rituals

I have thought a lot about pregame rituals and what works best for a team. And when I say pregame, that doesn't mean just arriving an hour and fifteen minutes before tip-off to get ready. Pregame for me starts at practice the day before.

It's there where we go over our scouting report on our opponents. It's also a time when I ask them to think about the next day's game that night before they go to bed. I want them to picture all of the things we practiced and prepared for. I want them to think of the next morning as Christmas Day — something they can't wait for because it's game day and they get an opportunity to play the game they love. It makes me feel great (and confident) when my players walk by and say, "Christmas Day, baby!" or "Merry Christmas, Coach!"

Things We Need To Do To Be Successful

I talk to my team day-in and day-out about the components that make a successful team — our defensive principles, offensive execution, attention to detail, team chemistry, and playing with heart and passion. These are constants.

In preparing for a particular opponent, though, I need to be more specific. For example, if we're playing a team that presses and traps all over the court, we need to be prepared to deal with that and know how to attack it. Your team needs to be ready for anything that your opponent may throw at you. This leads me to the next topic — knowing your opposition.

Scouting

Scouting is a tool to use in preparing your team for a particular opponent. I probably scout less than most coaches, but that doesn't mean that I don't think it's important. My goal in scouting is to have a general idea of what the other team is going to do and to know the individual strengths and weaknesses of their players. For example, I want to know what defenses the other team uses. Do they press? Are they a fast breaking team? Are they a perimeter shooting team? Do they pound it inside? Which individuals on their team shoot the best or attack the basket off the dribble? Can they drive with their weak hand?

I feel if I have this information, that's all I really need to know. I think it's more important to spend my valuable practice time on developing my own team. Again, I fall in line with Coach Wooden who said about scouting, "I will prepare my players the best I can and I'll let the other team worry about us."

In The Locker Room

Ok, your players had a solid practice yesterday. The game plan is in. At night, they thought about what they needed to do to be successful in their game, and they woke up thinking it was Christmas Day. Now what?

What's left is the actual pregame time. My guys arrive an hour and fifteen minutes before their scheduled start. Typically it's a 7:30pm tip off and there is a contest underway as we arrive.

When halftime hits of the game in session, my guys will come out of the stands and shoot around on the court. When our JV boys or Varsity girls come out of the locker room for the start of their third quarter, we will head back to the locker room ourselves to change into our uniforms, stretch out, and go over final instructions.

This is also a time where the personality of a team can really shine bright. Harkening back to my 2004 team, I had a young man, Johannes Demarzi, who was a natural leader. Even as a younger player, he got his teammates to gather around the piano (we happened to have one in our locker/classroom) and he would lead them in singing some sappy love song. This was their pregame ritual, and in its own weird way, helped get them ready for their game. I also think it unnerved our opponents a bit as well. They would walk by our door, peer through the window, and would be shocked to see our team singing together before the game.

Each year it's important to find the right style for your team. Some groups are very serious and want to prepare in silence. Others like it lighter and may want to listen to music. The most challenging squad is when there is a mix. That's when a coach really needs to check in with his team and make sure that the room is conducive for all types of preparation.

As a coach, what you bring to this moment is important. My aim is to be very confident and articulate. I also speak a little more quickly than usual. I believe my players retain more of what I say if I speak in a more rapid cadence. I don't want to appear nervous or overly excited. In doing so, your players will typically follow suit. I will restate our game plan and remind my players of our keys to the game. Sometimes I will share a story or something inspirational but generally I like to keep the same rhythm to our pregame.

What I don't want to do is stir my team's emotions into a frenzy. It's a mistake getting your players too hyped before the game. And with regard to rival games or "bigger" games, I want my players treating every game the same — we're playing a nameless, faceless opponent, and our goal is to play at our highest level.

Pregame preparation

A Little Bit About Attire

Coaches tend to fall into two camps when the topic of attire comes up. There is the more traditional — dare I say old school — mentality, which is a sweater, vest, or a polo shirt, often in school colors with logos, and there is the more formal suit and tie look. Both are perfectly acceptable. The most important thing is that a coach looks professional and neat, and represents his or her school appropriately.

Having said that, I am definitely a suit and tie guy. I feel it adds a little more of a special quality to the activity. Referees are always complimenting my suits. Rival coaches have called me the Pat Riley of high school coaches (Riley was considered the best dressed coach during his time in the NBA). My players like it. Heck, my wife likes it. Seriously, though, I see the impact it does have on my players. They dress up for their home games and many of their road contests as well. They even strive at times to outdress me. We have fun with it, but there's no denying it just heightens the overall experience.

Game Time

If you and your players have prepared properly, both on and off the court, the game will be the positive result of that preparation. It's a wonderful thing to see your players execute the game plan out on the floor. It demonstrates that what you are doing is working. The game will also tell you what part of your team development still needs addressing.

Timeouts

What can you do if your game plan isn't working? My best advice is to figure out why. A coach should be ready to make any needed adjustments during the course of the game. One way to do this is through timeouts. I personally don't like to use a timeout unless I have to. I want to save them for the end when I may really need them. I feel like my team is going to be the better conditioned team and taking a timeout will give our opponents an opportunity to rest and catch their breath.

Sometimes, though, a coach has no other choice. I will use my timeouts to stop a run from the other team, to diagram a play, to change defenses, or maybe just to try to get a little more effort out of my squad. During timeouts, a coach needs to be in control. He has to be very clear in his instructions to his team. Everyone needs to be on the same page, and if a coach has assistants, it's important that all the staff members know their roles. There's nothing more confusing than three coaches talking at the same time. For me, what works is: after I finish talking, my assistants add their input. Finally, don't give your team too much information. One or two suggestions is plenty. Any more than that, and you run the risk of your players forgetting everything you just spoke about.

Halftime

Halftime can be a big advantage if you use it wisely. How many times have you seen a team being soundly beaten make an incredible comeback after intermission? It happens. My 2019 team was a perfect example. It was senior night (last home game) and we were playing a strong opponent in Woodland Christian. From the opening tip we were a step slow, and Woodland was firing on all cylinders. We couldn't buy a basket and by the time the half ended, we limped into the locker room trailing 25-11.

As we got into the room we could see and hear Woodland Christian cheering and clapping as they ran by. They were already celebrating. At this moment, a coach has to decide what his team needs to hear.

Announcers on television, after a team makes a great second-half run to get back into the game, always comment that the coach must have really let his or her team have it at halftime. This is sometimes true, but definitely not always the case. I must admit there have been times where I lit into my team, but it has always depended on the circumstances and not the score.

The one thing I can't tolerate is lack of effort, and if my players are giving what I perceive to be less than 100 percent effort, you can bet they are going to hear about it. I believe this is okay from time to time if you have your team's trust and respect. In fact, my former players often recall those seven minute tongue lashings very fondly when we get together (I guess time does heal a lot).

Usually, though, my halftime talks are conversations with my players. My assistants and I will point out things that we can do a little better or things we can take advantage of, and my players will offer their insights into the contest, as they often give helpful input to our game plan. Using this time in this way will ensure that everyone on your team is unified and prepared for the second half of the game.

Back to the Woodland game. We are down 14, but I'm confident. We couldn't have shot any worse, but our defense had kept us within striking distance. I also loved the fact that Woodland was carrying on like the game was over.

I didn't yell and scream. In fact, I was very calm. I just had our guys make a few small adjustments with positioning in our offensive sets…and I might have had a couple of words about our opponent celebrating prematurely.

The third quarter started and we hit the ground running. We poured in a barrage of three pointers and their 14-point halftime lead was gone in four minutes. We outscored them 30-7 in the third period and turned a 25-11 deficit into a 41-32 advantage heading into the 4th quarter. Woodland was shell shocked. We stole their hope and any thoughts about winning almost immediately after the start of the third quarter, and cruised to a 57-42 victory — outscoring them 46-17 in the second half. We didn't know it at the time, but that win cemented our 4th consecutive league championship.

Here's another example on how halftime can play a role in eventual victory.

In Pat Williams book, *Extreme Winning*, Williams shared a story told to him by Steve Whitman, a former football player for the Alabama Crimson Tide. Whitman played for legendary coaching great Paul "Bear" Bryant. In this story, Alabama trotted into the locker room trailing the Tennessee Volunteers 17-0 at the half.

Whitman remembers that he and his teammates were met by Bryant walking back and forth gleefully clapping his hands and smiling. Whitman quipped, "He kept saying something like, "This is great! This is great! We got 'em right where we want 'em." Whitman and his teammates couldn't believe what they were hearing because they had been thoroughly outplayed by Tennessee. Whitman added, "I thought Coach had lost his mind. I thought that he thought that we were ahead. Then he started talking about how we had a chance to show what we were made of, a chance to show class. He said we had a chance to show a national audience what we were about. I don't think we talked much about strategy, other than Coach Bryant telling us our game plan was solid; that we just had to execute better."

The last thing Bear Bryant told his players was if they won the second half there was no doubt they'd prove they had what it took to win a National Championship. Then, just before he left the locker room, Bryant told them to sit and think about that for a few minutes.

Whitman said the players practically broke down the doors as they exploded out of the locker room, eager for a second half to start. The result was dramatic. The Tide dominated Tennessee and rolled to a 27-17 comeback victory. It pushed their record to 6-0 and led them to an undefeated National Title.

Don't discount how the right message and the right delivery can have a huge impact on your team. There is always more than one way to get your team's attention.

Post Game

As I mentioned earlier in this chapter with regard to structuring practice, it's important to finish the night with something positive. This is one of my main goals for my post-game talk. I typically start by getting the not so great parts of the contest out of the way. It's always important for them to hear about things we need to do better. I finish with pointing out the parts of our game that were strong or improving, and I usually acknowledge particular players for positive traits they exemplified.

There are rare occasions, however, when I may be hard on my team. Again, it comes down to effort and attitude. If my players aren't giving it their all, they will be held accountable. They need to know that effort is non-negotiable. There is no gray area. They will respect you more knowing that you hold them to their highest selves.

Now, if your team has done very well, it's important to appreciate their efforts, but also to keep it in perspective. I still want them to have their feet on the ground. There is always room for improvement.

One recent idea I've used with great success is "The beast of the week" award. This honor is handed out in our post game talk at the end of a week. This goes to the player that has demonstrated the best effort, attitude, and productivity throughout the entire week. The recipient gets to take the award home with him, put it up on his mantle in his bedroom all week, and then bring it back for the following Friday's presentation. My guys absolutely love this and it's proven to be a great way to finish a week.

Waves Beast of the Week Award

All in all, my goal in our post game talk is to not have my team too dejected over a loss or too elated over a win. I want them to be able to say they had played to their best ability, gave it everything they had, and I want them walking out standing tall.

Making Mistakes

Every coach is going to make mistakes, but it's important to differentiate between making mistakes and things not working. As a coach, you should make decisions based on solid reasoning. If they don't work, it doesn't mean they were wrong. An often stated sentiment (sometimes in jest) in coaching circles is, "I'm a much better coach when I have better talent." The reality is it's true. A coach can design the perfect play, the team can execute it properly, get the shot you want, but just not have the talent to make those shots consistently. This is an important element in evaluating your performance.

But, what if you do mess up? And what if it costs you a game? I remember watching a game that was for the NorCal Championship. The winner would advance to the state title. It involved two outstanding teams and two outstanding coaches. The score was tied with ten seconds to go and the coach of one of the teams called time out. The only problem was: he didn't have any left. Technical foul. Free throws. Ball game.

How does a coach deal with something like that? I believe honesty is the best policy. Admit it. Acknowledge it to your players. Let them know that you take full responsibility for the error. This will show them that you have confidence in yourself as a person and a coach and that you are not above making mistakes. Also, share with them your reasoning for your decision so they know how it came about. It happens to everyone. The more prepared you become, the less often it should happen.

I read the next day that the coach did take responsibility for the time out call, explained his thought process and apologized to his team. The players rallied behind their leader and let him know that he was the only reason they had gone that far in the first place.

Awards

Awards have become somewhat controversial at our school. The "anti" point of view is that awards single out the individual and that is something we don't want to encourage. Well, if that was all we were doing at our award ceremonies, then I would tend to agree with that statement. However, our award banquets are much more than that. We honor our teams with an evening that consists of sharing many of the memories of the season, a personal reflection of each player and what he or she meant to his or her teammates, and coach, and sometimes a gift (usually a team shirt) to each player.

The only individual awards given out for my teams are for traits that truly stand out. A few years ago, I distanced myself from the traditional most valuable player, most improved, and most inspirational awards. Nothing wrong with those, but I just felt like I wanted to freshen up the categories. I decided to create them myself. I now have awards like 'The Waldorf Way' for someone who embodies the spirit of a Waldorf player, and 'The Rising Star' for someone whose skills are really starting to take off. I even had a new one this year for one of my players that I called 'Mamba Mentality,' in honor of the late Kobe Bryant and how that award represented the effort, skill and tenacity that Kobe lived by.

Choosing Captains

This may sound like a little thing, but most players take this very seriously. Most feel it's a big honor to be chosen captain. Over the years, I have tried a little bit of everything when it comes to choosing captains. I have picked the same player(s) for the entire season, I have appointed different captains before each game, and one season I went the entire year without having any captains. It comes down to your players.

There are a few things to look for when choosing captains.

In my mind, a captain has to be someone other players look up to. He is a player (usually an upperclassman) respected not only for his skill on the court, but also for his outstanding work ethic. He is a leader and a positive role model to his teammates.

A coach needs to know that his captains will set a good example of how to carry oneself. What does it say about your team if your leaders are acting up in class, showing up late to practice, or getting into some kind of trouble outside of school?

Make sure you choose wisely, and don't make it an election. Your players may not be considering all the criteria that should go into this selection.

They may choose the best or most popular player without thinking about the other traits needed, and that may lead to problems for your team down the road.

Referees

In organized sports, referees or officials play an integral role. You can't play the game without them. They are there to help control and keep order during a contest.

I have built up a solid rapport with most of the officials in our area. I am a vocal coach and can be pretty animated on the sidelines on occasion, but I'm always respectful of the officials. They have a job to do, just as I do. If they know you aren't trying to show them up, you will almost always get a fair shake.

I expect officials to be on time, call a game consistently, hustle, and be in the right position to make the call. If they do those things, they will rarely, if ever, have a problem with me.

As a coach, it is your responsibility to make sure your players are respectful of the officials as well. Talking back to them or disputing a call is unacceptable. If you are modeling the right behavior, it should be easy for your players to follow suit.

Putting It All Together

There are a lot of aspects that go into preparing oneself to be a head coach — from learning the finer points of fundamentals, plays and strategy, to practice planning, motivating players, and developing a culture that embodies both your values and the school's — the challenges for a coach never end.

Make a list of the areas that you believe you need to be proficient in and lay out a plan to achieve that proficiency. There is great confidence in the feeling of being well prepared. I tell my players all of the time that I have given them the answers to the test, and they just need to go out and perform what they have been studying.

See yourself being successful in all phases of the job. The more you can put all of the different situations of a basketball program into your mind — and there are a lot — and truly visualize yourself being the leader that you want to be, the closer you will be to becoming the outstanding coach that is inside of you.

IS WALDORF BASKETBALL DIFFERENT?

You wonder why he does it
Striving to improve each and every day.
Look only to his work ethic
He knows no other way.

You wonder why he does it
It's all about being a Wave.
He has seen the players before him
And how their road was paved.

You wonder why he does it
Discipline and pride spells his name.
You wonder why he does it
He plays for the love of the game.

—Dean Stark

There is a lot of literature out there that explains why Waldorf education is unique. In *A Waldorf Approach To Coaching Team Sports*, I wrote about how one can approach sports and still align with Waldorf pedagogy. But specifically, how does one of my players' experiences differ from what a player from a non-Waldorf school gets?

There is certainly less practice, no cuts, less competition for a spot on the team, and no year-round specialization. We've already covered that. But what else separates the Waldorf hooper?

In preparing for this chapter, I asked my current players that very same question. I was curious as to what they thought. Here are some of their answers:

Tenacity, perseverance, and heart is what separates us.

Waldorf teaches us that anything is possible, and it's all about teamwork.

That not one person can solve a problem, but a group of individuals working together can conquer anything.

Knowing that you are a part of something special, and you're not just fighting for your team or school, but for past teams to uphold their legacy.

Our exacting attention to detail.

Our ability to fully commit to a goal and fight until we achieve it.

Our discipline sets us apart.

Our preparation for big moments.

All great answers and insights.

As in academic courses, all Waldorf basketball programs are not created equally. A brilliant teacher or coach, Waldorf or non-Waldorf, is certainly going to make a dramatic difference in the classroom and on the court. No one will dispute that. For clarity, this comparison can't come down to personnel. Therefore, leadership, expertise, and dynamism must be eliminated from the equation.

It's also not sportsmanship. As much as I like to believe that my teams always play the right way and are respectful to opposing players, fans, and to the officials — win or lose — there are many examples of exemplary behavior all over in the world of sports.

The typical traits that one hears involving athletics — heart, toughness, hustle, pride, commitment, and camaraderie — are not exclusively Waldorf traits either. So, what does that leave?

Is there a special quality left at the core of a Waldorf basketball player that separates him or her from every other high school player? Honestly, I don't think so. I don't believe it's one or two characteristics that no one else possesses.

It's virtually impossible to find something that is purely unique. Our art program at Sac Waldorf is extraordinary and yet there are non-Waldorf schools that have a solid art department within their curriculum. There will be some similarity.

We are talking about a sport that nearly all high schools field, and one that has the same rules and regulations. How different can it be?

Just because our program can share many overlapping characteristics with non-Waldorf basketball teams doesn't, however, mean that we're the same. In my estimation, the biggest difference between Waldorf players and players at non-Waldorf schools is not one or two special traits, but a combination of everything.

I believe a Waldorf basketball player brings more of these ideal characteristics to the table that coaches want to see in their programs.

It starts with time together. Most of our athletes grow up together. Being raised in the same community, having classes together from kindergarten on, playing on the playground, working in the garden, singing and playing an instrument together, and creating art and main lesson books.

It's watching the older kids on Friday nights and dreaming that one day that will be you.

It's bringing competition into their life at a time where they are most prepared physically, mentally, and emotionally to embrace it.

It's our coaches teaching in a way that fosters a love for the game.

It's having a balanced load in relationship to the rest of their lives. That, in turn, helps create a love for the sport and allows for their spirit to swell instead of drying up. It's committing their sport to their life instead of their life to their sport.

It's not one specific thing that makes us different. It's possessing all of what sports can be that makes the Waldorf experience stand out. We may not have the best team year in and year out — there will always be more talented teams. But for what a parent would hope that their child could experience in playing on a school team — camaraderie, sacrifice, discipline, goal setting, effort, and joy — I believe our Waldorf approach rises to the top.

Waves Basketball In Action

Dominic DeGennaro views his options

Tyson Duncan attacks the rim

Friday night fever

Christopher Olson puts it on the floor

Another "3" for Michael Bosque and the Waves

REMEMBERING JARRAD

To live in hearts we leave behind is not to die.

—Thomas Campbell

Jarrad Cole was larger than life. He was a strapping six-foot three-inch, 190-pound, 18-year old young man that was just beginning his next journey after high school, where he was a fixture on my teams from that era. He graduated from Sacramento Waldorf in June of 2007 and was set to start in the Fall at the Cal Maritime Academy in Vallejo, California.

Jarrad had a zest for life that I have rarely seen in my three-plus decades working with teens. That, in itself, is saying something because my days are filled with energetic and enthusiastic kids. Jarrad was different, though. He just seemed to have a unique ability to squeeze every ounce out of any moment and make that experience more memorable and special.

I can remember when our school was doing a community service outreach program and Jarrad was in my group. Our mission was to clean up different areas around the American River and a local park. During lunch at a deli in old town Fair Oaks, Jarrad shared with me that he could hypnotize chickens. I said, "Come on, Jarrad, you can't hypnotize chickens!"

Old town Fair Oaks just happens to be a mecca for chickens and roosters, so Jarrad said, "Okay Dean, you watch." Jarrad proceeded to walk across the street into a park and started racing after chickens and trying to capture one. To see a 6'3" giant chasing after these chickens, and to see the onlookers behold this with shock and awe was truly a hysterical moment that I will always cherish.

Fortunately, for the chickens and the startled observers, Jarrad didn't catch one. Knowing Jarrad, I'm sure if he did he would have somehow been able to hypnotize that bird.

This was just one tiny example of the exuberance that Jarrad brought to the world every day. As the starting center on my basketball team, Jarrad sported that same passion on the court. It was just simple things, really: his bounding in the gym before every practice with a huge grin on his face, eagerly awaiting its start, his walking out on the court right before a game's tip-off, striding up to the player he was going to guard, smiling, pointing his finger in the direction of that player, and saying, "I got you!"

He was also a young man who held great respect for his elders. One of my fondest memories of Jarrad was his actions on home game nights. Typically, my players arrive an hour and fifteen minutes before our tip off. They congregate in the students section at the far end of our gym, and watch our girls' game. My office is located at the other end of the gym — near the entrance to the court. I will go into my office, grab the ball bag, first aid kit, scorebook and whiteboard, and then head down to the far end to join my players.

Without fail, at first sight, Jarrad would leap from the bleachers, race down the sideline, grab all of my belongings as I exited my office, and bring them down to the other end for me. He wasn't kissing up to me. He wasn't vying for more playing time. He was just showing me respect and appreciation. I've coached hundreds of young men, but this act of kindness always moved me.

There are many other stories I could share about this special young man. He had a vast array of interests — hiking, playing the piano, singing, weight training, and he absolutely loved the Harry Potter books. You might be wondering, though, why am I singling out one player?

On August 4th, 2007 — just seven weeks after his high school graduation — Jarrad was involved in a tragic motorcycle accident that took his life. His bright and shining future was cut short in an instant.

The Cole family had a wake and a viewing in their home and it was the last time where we could spend a moment with Jarrad. Standing before him and seeing all of the 5x7 cards that I wrote to him about basketball and life on a table next to him hit me really hard. Those were some of his prized possessions.

To say our community mourned the loss of this great young man doesn't do his memory justice. I've never seen a time where so many were hurting so deeply. Jarrad genuinely touched everyone he came in contact with.

I was extremely honored to be asked by his family to speak at his memorial. I shared some of my remembrances of him — some that I mentioned here — and tried to paint a picture of how special he was and what he meant to us all.

As a school, we also decided to create the Jarrad Cole Award. This is an award that goes to a Sac Waldorf basketball player that best exhibits the traits that Jarrad both played and lived by. The chosen athlete gets his or her name engraved on a plaque that hangs in the lobby of our gym underneath Jarrad's retired No. 2 jersey.

The plaque reads:

Jarrad Cole Award

Embodies passion, camaraderie,

commitment, enthusiasm and excellence

in the sport of basketball

One of my greatest joys was being able to present this award to his younger brother, Sawyer, who earned the honor in 2010.

It has been almost 13 years since Jarrad's passing. I still think of him often and I feel blessed that I had the opportunity to coach him and share many moments with him. I have spoken about the manner in which he devoted his sport to his life regularly to my recent teams, and he is still an inspiration to me and a reminder to always strive to do more. There is no doubt that his lasting memory will continue to motivate me and countless others. His life was cut far too short, but it was exceptionally well lived.

I share this remembrance of Jarrad because I want to keep his memory alive. His life should never be forgotten. Hopefully, his story will inspire you to tell the people around you how much you love them as well. And don't put off tomorrow what you can do today. Tomorrow may never come.

PLAYERS AND RIVAL COACHES WEIGH IN

I have awed at a solo performance
And spectacular flashy display,
But I crave for the best
And my eyes are more blessed
When an unselfish team makes a play
A play that's so perfect and simple
With the weaving of role with a role,
Every piece parly seen
Like a fine tuned machine
And you notice not one but the whole
Like an orchestra tuned to perfection
Where harmonious beauty is found,
Every note has a quest
To be part of the rest
So the whole is a masterpiece sound
Every wild one once blinded by glory
Is now cured and is one of the tame,
He receives his esteem
As part of the team
And is eager to sacrifice fame
It's amazing what teams
Have accomplished
It's astounding how
Much they have done,

When the ultimate call
Is when one is for all
And the credit is reached by none

—Swen Nater

Henry Meier, Class of 2004

The first thing I tell anyone about my time playing basketball at Sac Waldorf is how our entire team would sing KC and JoJo's "All My Life" at the top of our lungs before every game.

This isn't *the* definitional experience of my time playing hoops in high school, but it does set it apart from just about everyone else's — we were an oddball bunch and, for whatever reason, belting out some R&B before going out to engage in physical competition both focused and relaxed us.

This ritual — which came about spontaneously during my sophomore or junior year — was somewhat of a departure from what was the real bedrock of our team success: preparation, dedication, and an unshakeable belief that if we executed and went flat-out for 32 minutes we could beat anyone we stepped onto the court with.

These maxims are almost universally extolled by coaches the world over. They are not, however, universally adopted by players. The singular reason the young guys I played with in high school bought into these core tenents was because our coach, Dean Stark, didn't just *say* these words, he *lived* them with absolute commitment. Instead of abstract concepts (what is dedication or preparation to a 14-year old?) we had someone in front of us who embodied everything he preached.

I don't think it was something I was explicitly aware of during my high school years, but in retrospect it's clear Dean's ability to teach holistically was a product of this commitment to these principles. He was prepared, he was dedicated, and he believed that if he executed and gave his all each minute he spent with us that success would follow.

His expectations for us were consistent with his expectations for himself. Were there times he was disappointed in us? Absolutely. Were there times he wanted to yell and curse at us? Almost certainly. Dean — always Dean to us, never "Coach" or "Mr. Stark" — always held us to his high standards, and there were times we fell short.

But in the 20 years I've known him — I began playing for him as a freshman in the 2000-01 season — I've never seen him break or lash out. He's famous among his players for his exuberant jumps and passionate stomps on the sideline, but his ability to compose himself and treat players with compassion and love in the most dire moments is unparalleled. To this day, whenever I stop by Sac Waldorf to play in an alumni game or to visit Dean in his office, he looks me in the eyes and I see someone who has dedicated his life to teaching young idiots like myself not just how to dribble a ball or break a full-court press, but how to live their life with honor.

This all makes Dean sound like some sort of saint-like guru — which ok yes he's *great* — but along with his principled ways and unyielding drive, he also has a brilliant wit and terrific sense of humor. I'm not sure this is something that is learned or can be taught, but one of the great joys of my time playing basketball for him was the downtime we were able to spend together and how we could always make each other laugh. For as earnest and intense as he could be when drilling us on a particular play or defensive scheme, he was able to turn on a dime and crack wise, which always gave practices and car rides to games a conspiratorial atmosphere. We were always in it with him; he was never aloof.

This is the stuff that sticks with me 16 years after I last put on a Waves' jersey. There are dozens of memories of games — particular plays, the crowd's roar, the high of winning, the crushing loss at the end of every season — and those are memories I cherish (yes, even those losses). But all those memories are remarkably insignificant in comparison to the deep sense of pride in putting in the work that Dean helped instill in me.

What is more remarkable is that I am just one of hundreds of players Dean has imbued these values in. During his 34 years at the helm of the Sac Waldorf basketball program, he's amassed 635 wins and 16 league titles, making him one of the most successful coaches in California state history by these measures. He's been honored as the California Interscholastic Federation's Model Coach of the Year and been given awards from both state and national sporting organizations. And yet if you ask him what his greatest accomplishment is, what his deepest motivating factor is in coaching, I would almost guarantee his answer would be is the impact he has on the kids that he gets to spend time with each season.

It takes exceptional grace to balance the duality of high school coaching. On the one hand, you're judged by wins and losses — as much as we might like to minimize it, winning counts — and on the other you are responsible for so much more when it comes to developing young kids as they transition into adulthood.

I am biased, obviously, but I sincerely believe Dean to be one of the true greats when measured on both accounts — something very, very few can lay claim to.

Christopher Tobin-Campbell, Class of 2006

Both good coaches and bad coaches are typically measured by the games they win and lose. What separates a good coach from a great coach, however, is quite different.

In high school, I was fortunate to be coached by one of these great coaches, Dean Stark. Dean has won more than 600 games as the head coach with the Sacramento Waldorf Waves high school varsity basketball team. I'm not sure how many games he's lost, but in the two seasons I played with him we lost a grand total of zero regular season games, and it seems every year his teams are either competing for or winning the league championship, so I wouldn't be surprised if his win-loss percentage is in the .750 range. Those are Mike Krzyzewski numbers.

In a Facebook post after his 600th win, Dean thanked his players saying:

> "To all of my players, past and present — winning 600 games is only accomplished in being around for a long time and having great young men to work with. I never could have accomplished this without your commitment, sacrifice, heart and skill. You all mean the world to me. Thank you."

It's one of the classic marks of a great leader, to give credit to the people he has led. And as much as I would love to believe that I'm part of some extra special group of people that made winning 600 games possible, it's obvious what the real common denominator is here. In fact, it's more likely that Dean took a bunch of ordinary individuals and helped them achieve extraordinary results.

What amazes me most is how the lessons he taught as a coach are lessons that transcend basketball: practice with a purpose, mentally prepare, work hard as a team not as individuals, do the little things well, set goals, it's better to be great at a few things than mediocre at many, etc. These are the principles you hear in leadership, management, and self-improvement books all the time.

Hearing these principles by themselves, they are usually easy to understand, but often quite difficult to put into practice: simple to grasp, but hard to do. What Dean gives his players is the rare experience of living by these principles, as well as a chance to realize the inevitable, extraordinary results that follow.

This experience is more valuable to each player than simply winning or losing any set of games. It's the kind of experience that sticks with you for life. You leave with an entire toolset of skills that you didn't have when you started, and the universality of the lessons learned allow you to draw on them again and again, regardless of the challenge in front of you.

Measuring this kind of success goes way beyond wins and losses. Not only has Dean changed the lives of the hundreds of players that he's coached over the years, but those individuals have gone into the world and shared their learnings with thousands more.

600 wins is something to be extremely proud of. It is proof that if you live by the principles he teaches, success will take care of itself, and I congratulate Dean on hitting this milestone. I also hope that he knows his success is not measured in the games he's won or lost, but in the lives he changed, and the impact on the world those people continue to have today. That is the true measure of a great coach.

Michael Farr, Class of 2007

My earliest memory of Waves Basketball was when I attended a playoff game at La Sierra High School. I was probably around ten years old. As I walked through the doors, it felt like I was walking into Madison Square Garden for a NBA Eastern Conference Final game. Standing room only. I still have images in my mind of players flying around, diving for loose balls. I don't recall who won, but that evening would impact the rest of my life. Waves Basketball and my infatuation with the Chicago Bulls sparked my love for the game.

Every Friday from then on, my Dad and I would travel to every Waves game near and far. I was young and would goof off a bit, but the majority of the time I was taking notes and stats on each player. I learned each player's name and they became my idols. Dean Stark was my Phil Jackson.

Fast forward to the end of my 8th grade school year. My love for the Waves and basketball had only grown deeper. I had set the goal to be one of the best basketball players Dean had ever coached. There was an energy about this team and I knew I wanted to be a part of the story. Dean gave me the opportunity to play summer league with the Varsity team. Dad and I had many conversations about this. This is exactly what I dreamt of and yet, I was incredibly nervous. There were less than a handful of Freshmen that ever played on the Varsity team. I was a nervous wreck off the court but as soon as the ball was tipped, I hit autopilot and had the time of my life. I had learned so much from watching Dean and the Waves for years.

Some of these lessons were passed down through what might be called tradition. These unspoken rules I later found out are more rare on other teams and difficult to find in life. With Dean there are no egos or privilege on the roster. The best players not only were the most skilled but were the ones that worked the hardest. This was never told to me but it became very apparent.

I was incredibly lucky to have had Henry Meier take me under his wing as a teammate, friend and mentor. Many of the things I learned and observed from Henry were passed down from Dean. He taught me how to be a Wave from the inside. "Be a part of something bigger than yourself" was the mantra that was driven to the team every year that I was a part of the program. This mantra seems a simple philosophy but difficult to find in other groups. I was lucky in some sense. I hated losing more than most so I was willing to take on whatever role was needed; passing up a shot, dive for any loose ball, and take a charge from the biggest player on the court — whatever was needed.

So many of the lessons I learned from Dean and Waves Basketball are a part of me and the career that I have built to this day. When I started with the Waves, I already had a burning desire to succeed and an uncommon competitive nature for basketball. My flame had no direction and like many youth, I did not always know how to use my efforts and energy most efficiently.

Do the small things well. Improve daily. Do just one thing a day that will help you improve or bring you closer to your goals. Consistently get better by improving the monotonous details. It's difficult to put into words all of the lessons, trials and tribulations I went through with Dean and the basketball program. I was a part of the Waves in one form or another for nearly 10 years. The most impressive thing about Dean is how he runs the team as a whole. He brings energy, focus and enthusiasm day in and day out, year in and year out.

I came back to assist Dean in coaching the Varsity Team for five years after graduating from Sacramento Waldorf. I had it easy. I could be the fun coach hopping into drills and helping the players that needed some assistance on their personal game. People should not overlook how difficult it is to coach large groups of people — let alone high schoolers — to work hard, play together and, more importantly, not allow their egos and personal interests takeover. Many Waves athletes do not know how good they have it unless they played for other coaches and programs.

Coaching with Dean was fun and amazing. What is remarkable to me is how he approaches the game. His preparations for practice and games is paralleled only by coaches in the professional ranks. His enthusiasm for basketball, coaching, and his team is unmatched. He cares not only for the team but for each individual player as an athlete and a human.

Many outsiders may see Waves Basketball as a small-school program that has some success. But if you look at the program and Dean as a whole, I think it is easy to see how truly incredible it really is. If we could dig deeper into what makes Dean Stark tick and analyze his brain and genetics, I think we would find many similarities between him and the greatest coaches on earth. In my world, Dean Stark is a name I bring up as my greatest mentor, aside from my amazing parents. He is a coach that belongs in the history books with Phil Jackson, Mike Krzyzewski and John Wooden.

Max Naylor, Class of 2009

My Senior year of high school will be a year that I will never forget. Not because of prom, or the Senior play, spirit week, Senior cut day, the classes I took, the friends I made, or prepping for college. This year will be remembered most for the time I spent on the basketball court, the road tips with teammates, the grueling practices with free throws and suicides, and most of all, the games played.

Tuesdays and Fridays were the best days of the week. Even better than the weekends. The team wore button down shirts and ties on these days, and that meant one thing: it was game day. I helped lead our team through a successful season that landed us in a situation where our last game of the regular season would determine the league champion. We faced Forest Lake, the biggest rival of ours during my time at Waldorf. We battled hard and lost the game on our home court by three points. I was devastated and full of anger, but I gained comfort knowing that, despite losing, we had still qualified for sectional playoffs, so there was more basketball to be played.

If there was one thing that I held more valuable than winning, it was the opportunity to keep playing basketball.

It was in these conference playoffs where my most memorable moment of high school sports took place. It was not just a moment for basketball, but a lesson for life that has stuck with me ever since. It was the first round, pregame, we were all in the locker room, and Dean was discussing the game plan with us as usual. He had a few motivation words of wisdom, and then he paused for a moment. He then addressed the seniors with something I will never forget.

I don't remember his exact quote, and it was probably more eloquent than this, but the message was:

> "There is no reason to give less than 100 percent. This could
> be your last game of your high school career. You don't want
> to regret anything. You don't want to leave this gym wishing
> you could have done more. You will remember this for the rest
> of your life."

That message was truer than I could ever have possibly imagined as a 17-year old kid in that moment.

We went on to win that game, and moved through several more rounds of playoffs before being eliminated by our dreaded league rivals, Forest Lake, in the Section Final Four. That loss was the single toughest loss of any sports game I have ever experienced. That was it. My career was over. Dean's words rang through my head as tears ran down my face in the locker room after the game. I would never play a high school basketball game again. Did I give it my all? Do I regret anything? Could I have done more? Is this really happening? All questions racing through my head.

That was 2009. Time has passed. Life has moved on and careers are underway. I am left with countless memories and two important principles from my years in high school basketball that I have taken with me through life.

First, if you are going to invest your time in something, work on it, hone your craft, and strive to become better; don't give anything less than your all. Time is a valuable thing. Sooner or later, it's going to run out. Not just for high school basketball, but for life. It is important to make sure you don't waste the time that is given to you. Make yourself better, make others better, and give 100 percent in whatever it is that you invest your time in. Don't wake up one day 30 years down the road and tell yourself you regret doing something, or not doing something, that could have made you, others, or the world a better place.

The second principle I've taken through life is: I hate Forest Lake.

Max Koehler, Class of 2017

A great thing about sports, or a terrible thing depending on your point of view, is that it is blatantly obvious how prepared you are for what is asked of you. I was not ready at the start of freshman year basketball at Sacramento Waldorf. In fact, I was woefully in over my head.

Going from 8th-grade basketball straight onto Dean's varsity team was an adjustment to say the least. I started to understand that reality when conditioning began, where on sprint three of 10 running up the hill that led to school, I was gassed. I finished all of the sprints, but my body was wrecked in a way it had never been before. In the timed quarter-mile that was required to make the team, it took me four attempts, and the mile and two-mile requirements took my best effort to get by. The practices were really intense too; Dean demanded we bring high effort in every drill.

We were a really young team, with only one senior and the rest of the group freshman and sophomores. Because of our youth and a spate of injuries, we were playing heavy minutes. That year was a whirlwind with a lot of growing pains. I enjoyed it, but it was really hard. I was expending more effort than I ever had in my entire life, and for a sustained period of time. Dean had very high expectations of us. If we messed up, he would adamantly let us know, but he was also as quick to acknowledge when we got it right. I think that season was when I started to understand what it meant to work hard, and what it takes to be successful. That was tested the following year.

In the spring of freshman year, I tore my ACL. I was out all of sophomore year. That was a hard year for everyone. The team was frustrated, Dean was frustrated, and we didn't win many games. It was a really important year for us though. For myself, having to battle back from my injury with rehab and going to the gym consistently made me a lot tougher — and a lot more focused. I think that the team as a whole understood what it was going to take to win games. Junior year was when the pieces fell into place. It's always interesting at the beginning of the season when you don't know how good the team is. It takes winning to make that apparent, and we were winning. More importantly, we were winning against good teams. It was tough for me offensively that year. I never entirely found my rhythm, but I felt different. The team felt different. We were tougher, more focused, and more connected. There's a confidence that comes from getting knocked down and climbing all the way back to be even better than before. It takes some character, and it takes a great coach.

I always believed that Dean was a great coach, it was one of the main reasons that I came to Sacramento Waldorf. I had seen the standings of the

Davis High School team, and I had heard stories from my brother who played there and my friends who were going there about the program. I didn't want that, I wanted to go to a program and a coach that had a winning culture. All someone had to do to see proof of that was to look up to the far wall when they walked into the gym and see the years our school had won the league title. Still, we hadn't been close to bringing the league title back to Sacramento Waldorf my first two years. It wasn't until Junior year that we really started to believe.

That year we saw in our play how Dean's coaching and style of play could be successful. The high expectations made sense because we were meeting them. The offensive sets made sense because we were getting great shots. The hours in practice devoted to defensive principles made sense because we were locking teams down. Before then, I never really liked the defensive side of the game; I didn't enjoy all the time spent in practice on defense, but by this point I loved defense. I think that a team's chemistry really comes out on the defensive end where it takes every man being at the right place at the right time. Even in my Senior year in games where I was hitting shots, it was the defensive side that resonated with me.

In my Junior year, it seemed that we were going to roll through the league, but it goes to show how in sports, the momentum can disappear in an instant. We dropped two games in a row late in the season, and beyond that we didn't feel right. It wasn't for lack of effort, focus, or preparation. The magic just wasn't there. Sports are like that, sometimes inexplicably, and things just feel off. The next game was one of my all-time favorites. With the league title on the line, we were down big at the half. It's games like these where the work and focus that the whole team has put in comes to the surface. We wouldn't have won that game the previous year. Instead, we climbed all the way back and won the game in overtime. It was a huge moment. That year was the first league title for the school in four seasons. It was incredibly meaningful. We made it all the way to the section finals. It still doesn't feel right that we lost that game.

That loss was a huge point of inspiration for me. My preparation for the next season started the second the final buzzer sounded. It was the first time that I'd ever begun preparation for something that far in advance. It's something that never would have even crossed my mind Freshman year. I would never have suffered through blistering summer runs in the California heat, or pushed myself in the weight room, or letting my parents know that I wasn't missing practices or games because of family plans. As I said before, sports show you clearly how prepared you are to meet expectations, and they also have a way of measuring how you've improved. By Senior year, in many aspects, I was unrecognizable compared to my Freshman year.

Instead of scraping by the mile requirement, I owned it, shaving off nearly two minutes from my Freshman year time. Instead of slogging through defensive drills, I embraced them, and by the beginning of league play, I felt that I could lock down the player in whatever matchup Dean gave me. I was in the best shape of my life. As a team we had that magic again, and we were winning. We played with an edge and a confidence that only comes when everyone on the team buys into working hard, showing up, making the right pass, and taking the right shot. I remember there was a week that Dean labeled a "character-defining week" against three good teams. Each of them was an incredibly close game, and in each of them, we were victorious. This time we did roll through the league, and we were undefeated league champions. I remember the feeling of sitting on the bench, knowing we were going back to the section championship, and I remember the feeling when we lost. At the time, that loss soured the season for me. There was no doubt in my mind that we deserved it more than the team that beat us. We felt prepared before the game, but sometimes in sports you're just off. Now, though, that game is just a piece of the story.

That we were able to have severe injuries, tough seasons, and gut-wrenching losses, to go through that and have two of the winningest seasons in school history, character-defining wins, two league titles, and a lot of great memories, speaks volumes about the program that Dean has created at the school, and how players respond to it. It goes beyond basketball as well. It's shown me how working hard persistently, diligently, and consistently for an extended period of time can have a profound effect on my abilities. It's given me confidence in myself that no matter what my goals are and how far away they may seem, I have it in me to reach them. Because I've done it before.

Gabriel Guzman, Class of 2017

When I think back on my experience playing basketball for Dean Stark at Sacramento Waldorf School, I am reminded of a time of battle, a time where being average had no place. I have countless memories of our team pushing beyond exhaustion in practice so that when game day came, fatigue wasn't an option. It was this mentality that Dean drilled into us from the beginning of preseason to the last practice of the year. Dean demanded 100 percent effort, no excuses, and no explanations. He accepted nothing but our best.

Dean Stark brought my Waldorf experience full circle. Before playing basketball, I had limited exposure to the world of competitive sports and, even more so, a limited understanding of what it meant to be disciplined and push myself mentally. Most importantly, Dean taught me the difference between passive participation and active competition. In sports or in life, when we merely participate, the results and experience we desire leave our control. When we compete, however, we do everything in our power to work towards a goal, and that provides us a level of fulfillment and reward that is unmatched. Playing basketball for Dean taught me the importance of competing not only in the game of basketball but in anything I do. He taught me to make no excuses and to perform at a level no less than my best.

Personally, there is nothing more painful than losing, and I can say with certainty that losing the section final my senior year of high school was the most painful moment of my life. However, as I've reflected on the moments and years of hard work that brought me and our team to that game, I see the powerful lesson that moment taught me. On that day, with the pressure, the hype, the history of our team, and the severity of the moment, I moved from an active component of our team's success to a passive one. Leading up to the game I was proud as team captain to have helped bring the team so far, yet unaware of the demanding task at hand requiring my full active engagement and execution to secure the win. Furthermore, through my shift in mentality, moving from active to passive, I let the outcome be determined by forces other than my own.

As I reflect on my journey in basketball, the section final loss stands as an example of what it feels like to go through adversity, and it is only through tasting it and understanding why that moment occurred that I have been able to move forward in my life with a sense of dominance, resilience, and fight.

I have countless memories of some of the happiest moments of my life playing for SWS — beating Delta to secure our placement in playoffs, going undefeated in league, and dunking on a fast break to set the tone and hype for the rest of the team. Some of these memories will stay with me forever. The memories that will stick with me most deeply, however, are ones that I can still taste. They are the painful ones, the ones that make my blood boil, and the ones that bring me back to those locker room moments where the only sound you could hear are the sobs of teammates as we soaked up what it felt like to lose it all. These memories are the ones that drive me to embrace any hardship at hand and fight harder than ever to never let complacency and mediocrity bring me back to those moments without a sense of pride for the effort I put forth.

Playing for SWS and being coached by Dean Stark taught me that the pain of making no excuses, pushing yourself through failure, challenging yourself mentally, and living a life in discipline, control, and resilience will never outweigh the pain of losing when you take a passive participatory position in life.

I can say with pride that after graduating from Sacramento Waldorf School, through my varsity basketball experience, I was prepared to go out into the word. I understood and had tasted what it meant to live in a world that only gives back to you what you put out. Through my four years at SWS, I pushed through adversity, I experienced what it felt like to always win, and what it felt like to lose when it mattered most. I carry this with me today — a chip on my shoulder and an understanding of what it means to have grit, to be the hardest worker in the room, to never leave the gym unsatisfied, and to take an active role in my life's success.

Most coaches don't take it personally when you don't give everything, Dean does.

Terry Battenberg, Sacramento-area Coach

My relationship with Sacramento Waldorf High School and Coach Dean Stark goes back 30 years or more. In the beginning, I knew very little about Waldorf School and their basketball program. I just recognized they were a smaller, private school looking to play some of the bigger basketball programs in the Sacramento Area where I coached. One season, the schedule in December left us with an extra weekend before Christmas. It was an opportunity for me to start a small, four-team tournament at my school, Ponderosa High School. One of the invitations I sent out was to Dean Stark at Waldorf, knowing he was interested in playing bigger schools. When he eagerly accepted the invitation, along with two other medium-sized schools, I was excited about hosting our first ever Holiday Classic at Ponderosa. Knowing Waldorf was a smaller school, I decided to schedule them in the first round so we would have a better chance of making it to the championship game.

That decision did not turn out too well for me or our team. Waldorf might have been a small school with a limited squad, but they had a couple of really good players who taught my team a few lessons that night. And let me add, they taught me a lesson or two also. We lost that game and moved to the consolation bracket, which is not a desirable situation for the host of a tournament. After that meeting, both of our teams went on to have their best seasons in school history, but Waldorf had the edge in bragging rights over Ponderosa, as well as several other bigger schools that year.

Soon after, I wanted to know more about this little school that had such a good basketball program. There was no doubt the players were well prepared, fundamentally sound, and gave their best effort during games. This was certainly a credit to their coach, Dean Stark, and all that he put into his program. I eventually learned that the school was a little different from most others in its requirements educationally. Everyone was involved in their studies of course, but also programs involving music and art, besides any commitment to extracurricular sports. As Coach Stark and I scheduled games and preseason scrimmages in later years, I noticed that sometimes players would even miss our competition or be late because of their role in a play or a musical production.

Several years later, I started a program at a new high school and was pleased that Coach Stark would agree to play my young and inexperienced team. He was quite gracious in hosting us and filling our schedule in those early years. It was at this time I learned that Waldorf did not allow practices during the first week of Christmas vacation. I had my teams take a few days off then too, but never a full week. Again, Coach Stark and his players always found ways to overcome the lack of action and still play great basketball after the holidays.

Toward the end of my coaching career, I had one more experience with Coach Stark's Waldorf team. I was, by then, also coaching at a smaller, private high school. We met in the semi-finals of the section tournament at a neutral site. Coach Stark had one really outstanding player that helped carry his team to a great season, but I had several excellent players and we won that meeting quite easily. In the end though, there was no denying that Waldorf did not fear the challenge and believed they could beat us. They fought to the bitter end and competed as Coach Stark wanted them to compete —tough and determined. It left a lasting impression on me that the Waldorf players, despite their rigorous studies, attention to the arts, and sometimes limited basketball practice time, could always play at the highest level against the bigger programs. This is not only a reflection on the players, their parents, and the school, but also on the leadership of their coach, Dean Stark.

Tracy McLaughlin, Sacramento-area Coach

I coached boys' varsity high school basketball in the Greater Sacramento area for 21 years and, during this time period, I faced the Sacramento Waldorf

Waves under the leadership of Coach Dean Stark on many occasions. I made every attempt to "strategically" schedule with Coach Stark toward the end of preseason, just before Christmas break. I always knew that his team would be in full-season form during preseason, when most teams would still be preparing. While many coaches would use the preseason to help build stamina for conditioning, chemistry for execution, as well as execution itself, Coach Stark's teams were always ready once the games began. This was just one of the impressive qualities of coaching that I admired and respected about his leadership. They were always very well-prepared, well-conditioned, well-disciplined, and extremely competitive. Whenever my teams played them, regardless of our success leading up to that point or our rankings at the time, we knew that we were going to be in for a tough fight. We learned it would always take our best effort to win. Anything short of our best effort would lead to us learning a valuable lesson. We learned quite a few lessons along the way.

I first encountered Coach Stark at a local Boy's and Girl's Club that he used for his home site. It was my second season at a private Christian school in South Sacramento. Our team had been winning, and my guys were feeling pretty good about themselves. There was a thin line that separated confidence from cockiness in high school sports, and my team was straddling the fence. I knew we were decent, but I didn't feel that we had been truly tested. When we arrived at the gym, the girls were in the middle of a game, so we had to wait for its conclusion. I did not see the boy's team. When I walked past a "small" gym, I heard shoes screeching across the gym floor. The screeching continued for the entire fourth quarter of the girl's game, up until just a few minutes before the start of our game. From the sound of their team's prolonged exercise, I knew that they were either going to be highly conditioned or grow weary as the game progressed. Once the game started, it became apparent that my concerns were validated, and that we had not been truly tested. The next 32 minutes further solidified my concerns, and completely changed the face of my program. Coach Stark's team hustled, scored, defended, and executed like a very well-greased machine. That same "screech" that I had heard earlier filled the gym for 32 minutes straight, only taking pauses for free throws and between quarters. They executed and applied relentless pressure as they ran us out of the gym.

The humbling loss provided me the opportunity to have my team's full attention at our next practice. We had just faced a highly skilled team that utilized all its tools, whereas we had been functioning as a group of individuals. I told them we were never going to compete with a team like that unless we changed our mindset and ideology. At the time, my guys wore the best gear a basketball player could have during a game; high-quality shoes, colorful socks, wrist bands, head bands, etc. Being from a small private school with a limited budget, they had purchased these items on their own. After this defeat, I instructed them to wear the same color shoes, same color socks, and no sweatbands of any type. From then on, we were going to focus on playing like a team instead of looking like one. I maintained the removed-accessories policy over the years. Coach Stark and his team were responsible for that. They had served us with a good ole-fashioned blue-collar whooping and fed us slices of humble pie. What I found more commendable was the humility that he and his team displayed in victory, which was a direct reflection of his teaching and leadership. It was just another tasteful ingredient he had taught his players to use on how to be a good winner. I have implemented several pages from his playbook of conduct for my teams over the years.

Being multifaceted in the coaching profession, perhaps my favorite attribute of Coach Stark's coaching ability would be his "in your face" man-to-man, fundamental, textbook defense. His teams would execute near flawless defense from year-to-year. Each team would be like a clone of any of his other teams. Although the players would change, the fundamentals, philosophy, and technique appeared to remain constant. Great coaches convince their players to buy into their philosophy to develop their program's design. Coach Stark's ability to do this has led to much success for his teams over the years.

I would utilize our contests against Coach Stark's teams as the "measuring" stick for how well we might fare in the upcoming season. If we played well against his teams, I felt confident that we would do well in the upcoming regular season and postseason. I also knew that we were going to learn lessons and redefine elements of our game that needed to be fine-tuned, because his teams would exploit our weaknesses, both offensively and defensively.

Coach Stark has set the standard for high school basketball in the way of discipline, work ethic, competition, and sportsmanship. After the close of the first private school, I coached at two other popular private schools in the area that played all schools from different levels. When asked who the best coach in Sacramento is in high school basketball, I have told many that it is Dean Stark from Sacramento Waldorf. He would be my first choice at any level. To achieve the success that he does year after year with different players is a credit to his coaching ability. Furthermore, he is a total class act and one of the most decent human beings you will ever encounter, of whom I am proud to now call my friend.

REGRETS, HEARTACHE, AND FLAT OUT MISERY

The ultimate measure of a man is not where he stands in moments of comfort and convenience, but where he stands at times of challenge and controversy.

—Martin Luther King, Jr.

Suffering is the true test of life.

—David Goggins

My wife got home from her hospital shift tonight (she's a pediatric nurse), and we did what we always do. We stepped into our outdoor barrel sauna before she even entered our home. With the coronavirus being what it is and my wife facing it everyday, we hope that if the virus did find its way on her clothes or skin the 194 degree sauna will destroy it. Certainly not a fool-proof plan, but every little precaution that can possibly help we are going to do.

As we sat in there sweating, she asked me if I had any regrets with coaching. I thought for a moment and then I realized this would be a great topic to speak about.

Anyone that's been in any profession as long as I have will have regrets. When the question was broached to me, a couple of thoughts came to mind pretty quickly. It's not as much regret, though, as it is just genuine pain and anguish. All coaches have felt it and here are some of my most painful moments.

Section Final Blues

I'm going to share with you the heartache of three section finals that my team ended up on the wrong side of the scoreboard. The first was in 1991. To this day, it's still the best team I ever coached.

We were loaded with talent and oozing with confidence. We had beaten three top ten teams in all of Sacramento and were ranked #2 in the state. We destroyed everyone in our league by an average of 70 points per game. I know that sounds like I was running up the score, but trust me we could have beaten teams far worse.

We sprinted into the postseason and beat our first two teams by more than 30 points each. At that time, there were only eight teams that made the playoffs so that already put us in the final. We would face Ripon Christian, the No. 3 ranked team in the state. This was also a time where the semi-final and the final were played at Modesto Junior College. That was a huge advantage for Ripon whose school was just down the road.

We were a pressing team and we jumped on them right out of the gate. It was 10-4 in the opening three minutes and it genuinely looked like we were going to blow them out of the gym. They were struggling to get the ball past half court. And then it happened. My second leading scorer and all around glue guy, Kris Seeley, who was crucial to our press, got an elbow under his chin. It ripped his skin open and he was lost for the game.

My regret was not asking if we could try to tape it closed and go get stitches in 90 minutes after the game. His dad was right there and a big supporter of our program. He was also a physical therapist. I just figured that he must know best and he wasn't saying anything. To this day, it is Kris's greatest regret as well.

Ultimately, the game continued and almost immediately my best player, Colin Poer, picked up two quick fouls. Both of these calls were highly questionable as well. We had to abandon our press, and with Colin missing chunks of the game due to foul trouble, and my second-leading scorer at the hospital, we couldn't quite get over the hump. We fought admirably but the section title slipped away.

It was a crushing defeat. It was one of those scenarios that everything had to go Ripon's way for them to beat us. There are still times when I think back to that game and get angry. I really believed then and still do that we deserved better.

Number Two

Fast forward to 2016. My team put together a great playoff push and advanced to the section final with a fantastic semi final win. This victory pitted us with Stockton Christian for the title. They were led by a college-bound, 6'8 post player that was a handful. We still entered into the contest very confident.

The game went back and forth the entire way. We were frustrated with how the game was being officiated. It seemed like every time we touched the big guy, the whistle blew. They were shooting an inordinate amount of free throws and as the action progressed, it was starting to take a toll on us. They ultimately shot 31 free throws that night to our 15. And them being a 60 percent free throw shooting team all season picked a great time to make 27 of them. That is virtually 90 percent. College and NBA teams don't do that…especially in a championship game.

With four minutes to go, we found ourselves trailing by seven points. The game was slipping away. Seemingly out of nowhere, my point guard Landon Wetterstrom caught fire. He scored on back-to-back possessions to cut the lead to three. With just under three minutes left and us surging, we get another stop on "D" and now have the ball and a chance to tie. Landon is feeling it and races down the floor and attacks the rim. He rises and then a Stockton defender slides in to try to take a charge. Landon shoots and scores. There's a whistle. I'm thinking Landon is going to the line with a free throw to tie the game. Stockton is reeling and we are on fire. But wait! No basket. The official waves off the bucket, calls an offensive foul which gives Landon his fifth — he has fouled out. Instead of being tied, in the midst of a 7-0 run, and having all the momentum, I lost my point guard and our mojo. We ended up losing the game by three and everyone was left with another "what if…"

I seldom if ever blame the refs for an outcome of a game. I was just filling you in on how it went. If there was a regret, it was just not being able to do enough to get this group over the hump. To see their sorrow and hurt in the locker room will always stay with me. I really felt like they deserved to win and did everything in their power to be champions. It just wasn't to be.

One Last Gutwrencher

Exactly one season later. We had to live with that taste in our mouth for an entire year. We were committed to getting back to the final and changing the outcome. We even had a camera crew following us all season filming a documentary on our pursuits.

We entered the playoffs as the No. 1 seed. We got a bye the first round and crushed our second and third round opponents. We didn't celebrate much. We were in the final again but this was where we expected to be. We were to face Sacramento Adventist. We had played them in the preseason at their place and snuck out with a three point win. We were trailing the entire game but made a furious fourth quarter rally and literally stole the game.

We knew they would want revenge and we knew they would be confident.

We, however, controlled the sectional final game from the start. We held the lead the entire first half and through the third quarter. Our advantage was seven going into the final eight minutes. They kept chipping away at us and scored to cut the margin to 1 with just over 1 minute to play. That's when the most pivotal moment happened. One of my players was fouled and he went to the line to shoot a one-and-one. On the foul, one of Sac Adventist's players fouled out. It just so happened that my guy who was going to shoot the free throws was now going to cover the new player entering for Adventist. The problem was that my shooter didn't know that.

Now I have been in this situation many times and in a tight contest, I don't want to talk to my player who is about to shoot. I want him to focus on shooting. I'm prepared to yell at him immediately after his free throw(s) and let him know what his responsibilities are. In my entire career, this has never come back to bite me...until this time.

My player misses the front end on the line, and, to Sac Adventist's credit, they advance the ball so quickly I couldn't get my shooter's attention on who he was supposed to guard. Their new guy is left open and he drains a 16 foot jumper. Suddenly, we are down 1. Again, to their credit, for a kid to come off the bench after sitting for a long time, and bury a shot the first time he touches the ball — with his team down one with a minute to go in a championship game...

Both teams go back and forth with opportunities in that final minute, but those were the last points scored. We lose by one.

This was a tough one as well. My team devoted an entire year to get back to this place and change the outcome. They suffered, sacrificed, and dreamed for a second chance, got it, and still ended with the same result.

Yes, it is a powerful example that hard work doesn't guarantee dreams coming true, and a perfect picture of sacrificing for the unknown. But my guys didn't want a teachable lesson at that moment. They wanted a section title.

I can defend my strategy and I can be critical of it. I consciously chose to not talk to my shooter before the play happened. I didn't want to distract him. I felt like I could still get the info to him because I always have been in the past. I wasn't able to.

Regret? I will say this. It has made me change how I will handle situations like that in the future. I'm not going to risk it. My players will always know who they are covering before the foul shot goes up. It's odd, though, it hasn't come up since.

These are three examples of regrets and misery. All different, but all deeply painful. When you coach long enough, you can't escape getting your heart broken every now and then.

Special Moments

Heraclitus, a philosopher born in the Persian Empire back in the 5th century BC, wrote about men on the battlefield — "Out of every one hundred men, ten shouldn't even be there, eighty are just targets, nine are the real fighters, and we are lucky to have them, for they will make the battle. Ah, but the one, one is a warrior"

If I was going to take the time to share some of my most difficult coaching experiences, I certainly am going to give the highlights of my career equal attention as well. It would be impossible to list or even remember all of the special moments I've had over my career at Sacramento Waldorf. Being at this beautiful place for 36 years has been an incredibly big part of my life. Teaching, coaching, mentoring, directing our athletic program, and sponsoring has been hugely rewarding. Trying to pick out a few instances that stand out has been exceedingly difficult, but I decided to narrow my focus in accordance to the theme of the book.

Championship Recollections

First, I've been blessed to be a part of 24 league championships in my career at Waldorf. 16 with basketball and 8 in baseball. Here are a few moments that truly rise to the top.

It was 2004. I had decided to return to coach the baseball team with co-coach Tim Connolly. I never thought I would step onto a baseball field again, but Tim's unbridled enthusiasm convinced me to grab a fungo and get back at it.

Our baseball team had struggled after the glory years of the late 80's through the mid 90's. We didn't even field a team for a couple of seasons.

But the Waves were back on the field and due to Tim's positivity, we had a great group of young men ready to compete.

Truth was, I did miss baseball. Coming back was a joy — especially working with Tim. To this day, he is still one of the two or three people that have influenced me the most in my life. He's an amazing example of modelling how to live one's life with pure integrity.

As our season progressed, we really started to play great baseball. We battled for first place the entire second half of league play. When we reached the final contest it was us and Forest Lake Christian sitting together at the top — all tied up. And, to make things more dramatic, they were going to be our opponent in the last game. It was us and them for all the marbles and they had to come to us.

It was a spectacular game that went back and forth and found us tied in the bottom of the last inning. We had the winning run on 3rd base in the form of Nick Heitzberg. Nick was a fearless, fabulous athlete who I had ultimate confidence in. There were two outs and we had a batter up that was clearly overmatched by their pitcher. I was coaching 3rd base and I noticed that their catcher was not keeping an eye on Nick after he caught the ball from his pitcher. He would just take it out of his glove and toss it back. I whispered to Nick if the pitcher threw a second strike, I wanted him to sprint towards home plate the very instant the catcher was about to throw it back to the pitcher.

Nick nodded his head, refastened his batting glove straps and took his lead from third. Right on cue, their pitcher fired strike two by our hitter, and as the catcher began to toss the ball back to his battery mate, Nick sprinted towards home. No one saw it coming. Nick and I were the only two on the planet that knew of our plan. As their pitcher was waiting to catch the ball, Nick was now flying towards the plate. Frantically, the pitcher caught the throw back and fired it right back to the catcher who was now trying to guard home plate. As the catcher received the ball, Nick lunged into a head first slide. A pile of dust…wait for it…"SAFE" yells the umpire. A dog pile erupts at home plate. The Waves are champions again. That's a good one.

Here's another.

In 2012, Chris Schwartz-Edmisten had put together the best individual season I have ever seen. He walked into every arena with a huge bullseye on his back and still managed to average over 34 points a game.

We came into that league season knowing that Victory Christian was the clear favorite. They had won the league the previous year and were returning four prominent starters. In the first meeting at their place, both teams entered the contest 5-0 in league. Chris played his typical out-of-his-mind game and carried us through three quarters. Early in the fourth quarter with us holding a precarious five point lead, Chris went up for a jumper and landed on his defender's foot. Instant pain entered Chris and instant fear entered his teammates, our fans, and honestly, our coach. I called a timeout to check on him. He gingerly hobbled over, grimaced in pain, tied his shoe a little tighter and said he was ok. I call an additional timeout just to give him a few more moments to recover. He went back out and literally limped his way to the win. With guys draped all over him and on one good leg, Chris still couldn't be stopped. He hit two big threes in the final four minutes, dropped 43 points, and put us alone in first place with a 61-53 win.

That was only round one.

In our second meeting, the Waves came in at a perfect 11-0 in league play. Victory Christian stood at 10-1. We win, we are undefeated champions. In the locker room, I remember sharing with them that we are already champions. The question is do we want to share it? And, do we want to do what (at that time) only five other Waldorf teams had ever done — go undefeated in league? The resounding answer was yes. But, we had a big obstacle in front of us. Victory was a veteran team that knew what it felt like to be champions.

The place was packed. To this day, it's the most people to ever witness one of our games. The fire marshal would have certainly shut us down. There wasn't an available seat or anywhere else to stand.

From the tip, Chris was, well, Chris. Regardless of what they threw at him, he and we had a counter. At halftime, we led 34-32, and after three quarters we had widened the gap a bit to 54-49.

The fourth quarter was crazy. Both teams desperately wanted it. This was a game that someone had to take. Nothing was going to be given. Victory relentlessly came at us all quarter and finally tied the score at 67 on a driving layup with 40 seconds remaining. Chris didn't blink. Facing full court pressure, he brought the ball up while being closely guarded on the left side of the court. Soon after he crossed half court, he suddenly pulled up for a deep three. I think it caught everyone by surprise. Shooting a three off the dribble from that far out is very risky — especially in that situation. For anyone else I have coached, it is a bad shot. Not for him…Splash!

With their title hopes slipping away, Victory raced down the floor and fired up a rushed shot. We rebounded the errant attempt and quickly got it into Chris's hands. Fouls and free throws came next, as Chris knocked down four in a row to seal the win and give him 40 on the night. A truly spectacular performance. Final score Sac Waldorf 74 Victory Christian 67. The Waves are undefeated champions again.

One Final Shining Moment

In 2018, we were coming off one of our greatest seasons. My 2017 team was dominant. We won 27 games, dismantled our league, winning all 14 games by double digits, advanced to the CIF Section Title Game, the Final Four of the NorCals, and finished the season ranked No. 3 in the entire state.

For 2018, we had to replace six graduated seniors (including four starters), and we returned only two players that got meaningful minutes from the previous year. This season was supposed to be the one where the league gave us a little payback.

My guys, however, weren't going to relinquish their champion status without a fight. We struggled early on in our preseason and at times it really looked like we were in for a long season. In fact, on Dec. 12, we lost a hard fought double overtime game when a kid from the other team threw in a desperation three-pointer at the buzzer. The defeat left us at four wins and five losses on the season.

That game, though, ignited a run that none of us could have imagined. We reeled off five straight wins to finish the preseason, and headed to our league opener with renewed confidence and a title to defend.

We continued our strong play and went through the first half of the league undefeated. Our winning streak now stood at 12, and we had no intentions of stopping.

The second half of conference play, as always, proved extremely challenging. We were tested each game, but somehow managed to escape every encounter unblemished. After outlasting Futures 47-45, we had put ourselves in a great position. We were 12-0 in league and were headed for rival Foresthill, who came in at 11-1.

With only one game remaining following our Foresthill tussle, we knew if we knocked them off, we would clinch another league title. But this wasn't going to be easy. Foresthill was searching for its first ever conference championship and they knew they were only a win away, on their home turf, from probably achieving it.

And their home court was a huge advantage for them. From their often rabid fan base, and their seemingly tight rims, it's always hard carving out a win there. This game would be no different.

From the opening tip, it was a playoff atmosphere. The stands were filled with Foresthill faithful and I had never heard them so loud. It was awesome.

To make things more interesting, my starting center, 6'5" Tyson Duncan was out with an injured thumb, and his replacement 6'4" Chris Olson was battling the flu. We were short handed, but undeterred.

The game was tight from the onset. Points were hard to come by for both teams. Neither team could separate from the other and at halftime, the score stood at 21-18 in favor of Foresthill.

The second half was no different. Each team was fighting with tremendous effort. Both squads dreamed of championship glory.

We took a slight lead 38-36 entering the fourth quarter and as the game came down to the wire, Foresthill scored on a rebound putback to take a 44-43 lead with time running out. I called timeout to set up our final play. I wanted our point guard, Saahil Bhakta, to go off of a ball screen and look to attack. Foresthill double teamed Saahil, however, so he had to give up the ball. He found our shooter, Dominic Degennaro on the right wing. The clock was now down to three seconds. Dom didn't have space to shoot so he attacked the baseline. As he was going up for a shot, he saw our forward, Hunter Lowery, on the weak side block battling for position. Dom somehow shoveled the ball to Hunter and as Hunter went up, he got hammered by a Foresthill player. Foul — with 0.3 seconds left.

Now Hunter has to go to the free throw line with the raucous hometown crowd yelling as loud as they possibly can. Before the official hands Hunter the ball, though, Foresthill calls time out. They want to ice the shooter.

This is a great time to share with you that Hunter is a 49 percent free throw shooter. Throw in the significance of the moment — a league championship on the line, the boisterous crowd — and the odds of him making just one are fairly slim.

Timeout is over and Hunter steps back to the line. The crowd gets into a frenzy again. The ref hands Hunter the ball. Dribble, dribble, dribble, gather, spin, wrist cocks back, release…Swish. The game is tied. Timeout, Foresthill.

My guys ran back over to our bench. Defensive stopper Patrick Ku nearly body slams Hunter because he's so excited. "Don't celebrate," I screamed. "Stay focused."

Foresthill is trying to ice Hunter again with this timeout. We break the huddle and head back to the key. Hunter walks to the line again. The score is 44 all. There is 0.3 seconds on the clock. The fans start screaming again. The ref hands Hunter the ball. Dribble, dribble, dribble, gather, spin, wrist cocks back, release...............SWISH.

Foresthill grabs the ball out of the net, passes it inbounds and one of their players throws up a desperation heave that's not close and wouldn't have counted anyway. The game ends and we swarm our little area of the court. We are champions again!

But, the story doesn't end there. My players run to the locker room as I go hug my wife and daughter. As I join my guys a couple minutes later, I enter into a scene I've never experienced in my coaching career. I have multiple young men crying uncontrollably. I honestly got teary just now thinking about it. It literally took five minutes for a number of my guys to gather their emotions.

These tears of joy were not for winning another championship. It was much more than that. The crying was for what this championship represented to all of those seniors in the room. For Jun Kawano, for Saahil Bhakta, for Patrick Ku, for Hunter Lowery, for Jonas Poer. Yes, they were a part of an undefeated championship season the year before, but almost all of them played a much lesser role on that squad. This title was theirs.

And not only did they cap off a perfect 14-0 conference record in their final league game with a win, their first round playoff victory gave them 20 consecutive wins — a Sac Waldorf record. They didn't lose a game from December 12 to February 24. Magical!

RETIRE OR REDEFINE

Men do not decide their future. They decide their habits, and their habits decide their future

—Mike Murdock

I can remember back in the early 2000's our High School Administrator at the time, Tim Connolly, and I talked about retirement. I told him that I didn't want to be one of those old coaches that just rolled the balls out for practice, and slumped down on his chair watching as the game passed me by. I didn't want to hang on, win my 700th game and have my school give me a gold watch and a shove out the door.

Now here we are. I'm sitting on 635 wins. I am only 25 away from tying the record for most wins in CIF Section history for basketball boys or girls. That is one spectacular season or certainly two average years away. And after those two years, I could potentially be looking at one or two more seasons needed to reach 700. No CIF coach has ever done it.

This is where legacy steps in. I never started in this profession with any long term goals. No set number, no thoughts of multiple league championships. I certainly wanted to win, but mostly just wanted to make the experience special for my players. In fact, I never knew how many wins I had until someone asked me during the 2003 season. I started counting and it was then that I realized I could reach 300 that very year. Well, I did, and

I have never been able to escape my win total since. It has a way of kind of haunting you.

So if and when I surpass the 660 mark, will I want to coach the couple more years to hit 700? Right now I can't say for sure. I will be honest…I do want to be the winningest basketball coach in section history. I do want to be the first coach to ever win 700, and I do believe it would cement my induction into the CIF Hall of Fame. Those are big things and those are big dreams.

But not at any cost. I also want to respect the game and make sure I'm coaching for the right reasons. I couldn't imagine coaching any other way than I do right now — the way I've done my entire career. I'm all in and living and dying on every possession. I have great passion for this game and it's of the utmost importance that I'm giving my players an incredible experience. I still believe that I am a powerful motivator and I like to think that my relationship with my players is still deep, respectful, and even loving. I also still have a burning desire to improve. If I can still honor these characteristics that I value, and help create magic moments for my players, I can see myself continuing.

There is one other part of this equation, however, that I haven't spoken about until now. In 2015, I got married to an incredibly special woman named Aimee. She and her (now our) daughter Famy are the biggest part of my life. They have already been through the trials and tribulations of having a husband and father that coaches basketball for a while now. They are my world and I also want to make sure they are cared for.

There's no way of getting around it, but there will be times when I'm a little stressed during basketball season. Aimee feels the pressure watching the games from the stands as well. It's a lot to take in and I want to make sure that they are on board as well.

We love to travel and basketball coaches are never able to during the season. It always means that Thanksgiving and Christmas trips are out. I know she misses those opportunities.

For now, though, I have their support. In fact, Aimee is now my volunteer assistant in our off season conditioning program, and loves training with the guys herself. Truth be told, she likes seeing me on the sideline.

Even after 34 years, I'm still striving to get better, my fire is burning, and my players are having a great experience. As long as these things stay in place, I plan on continuing to coach this game that has given me so much, and that I love so deeply. Go Waves!

My wife Aimee and I share an embrace after a game

Pretty cool milestone!

CONCLUSION

What counts in life is not the mere fact that we have lived. It is what difference we have made to the lives of others that will determine the significance of the life we lead

—*Nelson Mandela*

What do you say to a community that has given you so much in your career that you couldn't possibly repay it all? That's how I feel. I embarked on this journey as a 21 year old man having no other vision than stopping off at this small school to gain some valuable experience before making my next leap.

I never could have dreamt that the valuable experience I would receive would expand to an entire career. To say I've been blessed doesn't nearly do justice to the fulfillment I feel.

My career starts and stops with my students. Allowing me to be part of their lives as a teacher, sponsor, and coach presented me a road to impact young people's lives. I jumped at it and followed that path for a time that is now inching toward 40 years. I know of no other occupation that can fill someone with such energy, enthusiasm, and hope.

As I reflect on what has been, I feel great satisfaction in living a career loaded with service and purpose. To ponder what is still in front of me and honestly be excited about it is truly more than I can ask for.

There will be a time for me to step away. A time to retire from teaching and coaching. When that day comes, I do believe I will be ready. I have studied many of my colleagues and how they have moved on. I want to get it right.

Until that day comes, however, you best better believe that I will still be squeezing every ounce out of life. One of my favorite quotes comes from Joe Dimaggio, the former baseball great. A reporter once asked him, "Joe, you play in over 150 games a year, and have over 600 plate appearances. Yet, every time you put the ball in play, you run it out as hard as you can — even if you have no chance of making it. Why?" Joe stared at the reporter and replied, "Because there might be some kid watching me play for the first time. I owe him my best."

Words to live by.

Peace

THE POWER OF THE WAVES

I've written often in these pages the blessing it has been to work my entire career in the Sacramento Waldorf community. Even as I write this book, the gifts continue to unfold for me.

In reaching out to past players for their remembrances, opportunities have come pouring in to help this project along. From my '04 former star center, journalist, writer and editor Henry Meier taking on the editing of this book, to '96 tenacious power forward Noah Klocek, a Production Director at Pixar (most recently with the 2020 movie 'Onward), providing the cover art, and finally to '93 silky smooth shooting guard Jeff Dorso, senior Vice President and General Counsel of the Sacramento Kings, for his unyielding support and in helping to guide me through the publication process, the voices of Waldorf past live as strongly within me today as they always have.

To my players, students, colleagues, alumni, and the entire world that is Waldorf, I humbly thank you again for the deep impact you have had in my life.

AWARDS AND ACCOMPLISHMENTS

2nd most wins in CIF Section History (635)

16 Central Valley California League titles

17 CIF Section Final Fours

2017 NFHS California State Boys Basketball Coach Of The Year

2017 CIF State Model Coach Winner

2017 CIF Section Model Coach Winner

16 Time CVCL Coach Of The Year in Boys Basketball

Sacramento Bee's 2010's Boys Basketball All Decade Coaching Staff

Author of *A Waldorf Approach To Coaching Team Sports*

Producer of Video *The Seven Defensive Principles Of Building A Championship Team*

REFERENCES

Carroll, Pete, *Win Forever*. New York: Portfolio/Penguin, 2010

Pitino, Rick, *The One Day Contract*. New York: St Martin's Press, 2013

Holtz, Lou, *Winning Every Day*. New York: HarperCollins, 1998

Armstrong, Lance, *Every Second Counts*. Broadway Books, 2003

Goggins, David, *Can't Hurt Me*. Lioncrest, 2018

Smith, Dean, *A Coach's Life*. New York: Random House, 1999

Sarno, John, *The Mindbody Prescription*. New York: Grand Central Life and Style, 1998

Sachs, Nicole, *The Meaning Of Truth*. Delaware: Safe Harbor Press, 2016

Stark, Dean, *A Waldorf Approach To Coaching Team Sports*. Rudolf Steiner Press, 1999

Steiner, Rudolf, *Education For Adolescents*. New York: Anthroposophic Press, 1921

Williams, Pat, *Extreme Winning*. Florida: Health Communications, Inc, 2015

Afremow, Jim, *The Champion's Mind*. Potter/Ten Speed/Harmony/Rodale, 2015

Wooden, John, *They Call Me Coach*. New York: Bantam Books, 1973

POSTSCRIPT

It is inching closer to November and this manuscript is headed to print very soon. A lot has happened since I sat down to write this book back in March. Due to Covid-19, our basketball season starting date has been moved from Nov 2 to Feb 22. Our section is doing everything in its powers to salvage sports, but it's impossible to not feel like it's starting to slip away. When Division 1 college programs are shutting down their seasons, believing that high school athletics will somehow survive is becoming harder to wrap one's head around.

I have to hand it to my team, though. We took on our Misogi challenge and handled it like champions. If you remember, our goal was for each person to complete at least 333 individual workouts in a 20 week period. That averages out to roughly 2 ½ workouts per day. This would also have put our team at 4329 total workouts - a truly impressive number. However, not only did we hit that mark, we obliterated it. On Sep 7, our final tally totaled 6271 training sessions. We beat it by close to 2000. My players averaged just under a whopping 3 ½ workouts per day for 140 consecutive days. Just an unbelievable accomplishment!

In great Misogi fashion, I designed a shirt for their efforts. It says Spirit of Doryoku which translates to unsurpassed effort.

I am so proud of these young men and the commitment they have shown to me, their teammates, and to themselves. The future promises them nothing, but they are still hoping and preparing for the possibility that they will get to step on the court again and represent our school.

This experience has truly embodied the sacrifice for the unknown theme my teams have modeled all these years. Whether they get to compete or not, this group has gained so much from tackling this challenge.

I asked them all what was their greatest takeaway in taking on this Misogi challenge. Here are some of their responses:

How to lead a completely self structured lifestyle.

Learning how to discipline myself to get work done even when I don't want to.

It helped immensely with my procrastination.

My Misogi gave me the drive and will to execute and accomplish my goals.

It pushed me to my limits and it allowed me to prove to myself that if I wanted something badly enough, I had it within me to reach it.

Competing our Misogi as a team offered ultimate competition, and it brought our team closer together.

I found the blueprint to making my dreams and goals come true.

As you can see, I have a special group.

Below, I'm sharing with you our 2020 Misogi Challenge.

I encourage you coaches out there to create your own with your team, and I would also love to hear about it if you do. It literally can be a life changing event.

Misogi Challenge

Guys,

Our off season work ethic will define our year. Taking on this challenge is going to be very demanding. Many of you will want to quit. Twenty weeks is a long time. Often, it's not going to be fun. The fun will come, though, when the work is done. The reward is on the backside. Do you want to be a better player? Do you want to be a special team? If so, you need to put in the time and endure the pain. As David Goggins says, "Suffering is the true test of life."

If we embrace this challenge and stick with it, we will be an unbelievably tight knit group. Our collective hard work is what will separate us from other teams. My dream is to have all of us totally commit. Before 4/20, text me with the words "All In" to let me know you are ready and excited for this endeavor.

Beginning April 20, there will be 140 days until September 7. Make a calendar like we did in our conditioning group, and mark off your daily workouts. I will log your totals each Sunday night on our zoom chat. I understand that not all parts of your

Misogi may be physical training. But for the ones that are, keep track of them.

One final word - It's possible to do over 400 physical workouts in these 140 days. Remember, a Misogi is taking something on that you don't know if you can do. Also know that the number of sessions achieved isn't as important as the level of intensity. I can see all of you working most days on basketball skills, yet playing 'horse' isn't a workout. Push yourself to be uncommon.

To the one who completes the most training sessions (each workout has to be legit), he will be presented with the first annual Spirit Of Doryoku Award. The term Doryoku is Japan's most highly prized virtue. It stands for unsurpassed effort. It's pronounced - Door-e-o-ku. This will be an incredible accomplishment. Also, if the combined total number of workouts for our team is 4330 or above (13 players and 333 workouts per person), you will be treated to an incredible feast at the Arigato Restaurant to celebrate your achievement. This would be an average of 333 workouts per player. Bam!

In keeping with this theme, the level of the categories will be defined by the ranking of Japanese fighting warriors:

Above 350 training sessions - Samurai

300 349 - Sohei

275-299 - Ronin

Under 275 - Ashigaru

Okay, we have our mission. Now let's go be spectacular!